VIVAT! VIVAT
REGINA!

Vivat! Vivat Regina!

A Play in Two Acts

by

ROBERT BOLT

HEINEMANN
LONDON

Heinemann Educational Books Ltd
LONDON   EDINBURGH   MELBOURNE
SINGAPORE   JOHANNESBURG
IBADAN   HONG KONG
TORONTO   AUCKLAND
NEW DELHI   NAIROBI

ISBN 0 435 23104 9 (cased)
0 435 23105 7 (paper)

**All rights whatsoever in this play are strictly reserved
and applications for performances, etc., should be
made before rehearsal to Margaret Ramsay Ltd,
14A Goodwin's Court, London, W.C.2.
No performance may be given unless a licence has been obtained.**

Published by
Heinemann Educational Books Ltd
48 Charles Street, London W1X 8AH
Printed in Great Britain by
Morrison and Gibb Ltd, London and Edinburgh

CONTENTS

Introduction   vii
A Note to the Designer   xxv
Principal Characters in order of their appearance   xxvi
Cast of First Performance   xxviii

VIVAT! VIVAT REGINA!

ACT ONE   I

ACT TWO   57

INTRODUCTION

The writer of an historical play is a kind of playwright, not a kind of historian. But I think he is obliged to be as accurate, historically, as he can.

He has borrowed not only his story but some of his emotion from actual people who actually lived. He is in debt to them for their virtues and vices, imaginatively energized by the actual energy they expended. He owes them the truth and is a kind of crook if he doesn't pay up.

Then too, the audience brings a special credulity to a history play. They credit the events they see enacted with a degree of actuality not claimed for events—like Shylock's bargain—which are purely theatrical. We are additionally moved when an actor plays out the noble death of an historical character by the knowledge that some such person did make some such death. And the playwright exploits this. Because everybody in the audience knows that Joan of Arc really was executed the playwright can take her to her death with an authority and an appearance of inevitability which he would otherwise have to work for. He can only honour this double debt to his characters and to his audience by sticking to the facts.

To what extent is this a restriction, an abdication from creative freedom and responsibility?

Well in the first place, historical facts are imperfectly known, even important facts about important people. On the evidence available we cannot know for certain (though few historians doubt it) that it really was Bothwell who murdered Darnley, or whether Mary married Bothwell willingly or was abducted. Still less, on the evidence available, can we know what it was that kept Elizabeth unmarried to the end.

The further back in time we go the less evidence there is. The further we come forward the more evidence there is. The surviving evidence for the reign of William the Conqueror could be arranged on a kitchen table. The evidence for the year 1970 would fill a warehouse. The historian who wishes to write a readable history of 1970 will have to ignore most of the evidence available, selecting only those facts which seem to him important and making sensible connections between them. His orderly account of last year will not bear much resemblance to the confusion of last year as we lived it. But that is why we value his account. That warehouse full of old newspapers is simply so much rubbish and might as well be burned. It bears only too much likeness to last year as we lived it. It is the difference between history and life which gives history its value, and the difference is creative.

It is the great good fortune of the historian of William the Conqueror that time and chance have so thoroughly winnowed the evidence for him. He can hunt for fresh evidence secure in the knowledge that he will not find it. Or at best will find only so much of it as will set his creativity to work anew. As a disinterested hunter of the fact he can claim to be a sort of scientist. Yet knows he must remain a sort of artist.

No, the playwright does not bind himself to anything constructed of cast-iron when he binds himself to history.

Of course I couldn't write a play in which Mary Stuart was a virgin and Bothwell ran off with Elizabeth and claim it was historical. There are limits.

But if the playwright finds the limits limiting then he is writing the wrong play. If he is rightly in love with his subject then the facts—even those which do not fit his preconceptions or which fit least readily upon a stage—will present themselves as opportunity and stimulus, not limitation.

More properly it is not his subject which the playwright loves but the play he hopes to write about it. More properly yet the playwright has a latent love for the play *form*, which he hopes will crystallize about his subject; he has in his heart a play-shaped vacancy which he will fill now with his subject.

The filling process will be strenuous. The subject, though it is not cast-iron, yet it does have a shape of its own. And the play form though it is flexible yet it does have limits too—my goodness has it not. But so has every form. Painters at their work will curse the disabilities of paint. But it is only because of what paint will not do that it can be got to do what it sometimes marvellously will. If paint could do everything then only God could work with it and paint would be the substance of the Universe instead of what it is, an artist's material. All forms of art derive their power from their limits and the artist finds it so.

That is not to say that he finds it agreeable. I cursed plentifully as I cast about for ways to accommodate the facts about Elizabeth and Mary in the form of a two act play.

The most obvious problem was that of sheer length, I was to collapse the events of twenty years into three hours.

The next difficulty was that my two protagonists never met. Schiller in his play invents a 'secret' meeting in Fotheringay Park. But the fact is that the two never came within a hundred miles of one another.

And then their two stories were so different. Mary plunged to final disaster by a pell mell succession of passionate actions, by expense. Elizabeth rose cautiously to her final triumph, by accumulation, mistrusting action.

I found their individual stories merely sad. But when I put the two together a theme seemed to emerge with uncanny clarity, as though they had been put on earth to illustrate it. The theme is Power, the pressures and the penalties of Power, the gap between the fine appearance which Power makes and the shameful shifts by which it is sustained. Above all the unnaturalness of Power, the impermissible sacrifice of self which Power demands, and gets, and squanders; to what purpose?

Elizabeth, a legendary political virtuose ('She alone knows how to rule!' exclaimed the cynical Henry of Navarre in a rare moment of enthusiasm) lived to be old; and hideous; and so neurotically deprived that all her courtiers, greybeards and boys, had to go through the motions of being in love with her.

Mary was a legendary femme fatale. Her portraits do not show by our standards a beauty but her contemporaries, friends and enemies alike, agree that she was irresistible. 'The finest she that ever was' reported one hostile emissary to Scotland. And another, reeling from an early interview: 'What a princess, what a lady!' The young French courtier-poet Chastelard from the death cell (where he had been sent for hiding in her bedroom) wrote: 'La plus belle, et la plus cruelle . . .' Yet the brilliant creature, once Queen of two countries—some thought three— died alone and in prison, unwanted and helpless.

They are figures on a see-saw, so similar and opposite. They were enemies but mutually fascinated. Each wore the other's portrait in a locket.

Elizabeth wanted to marry only one man in her life, the dashing Robert Dudley. But Robert Dudley fell under suspicion of murdering his wife. For Queen Elizabeth the mere suspicion was enough to prevent the marriage. Bothwell really did murder Mary's husband, yet Mary married him, and ceased to be a Queen in consequence.

Then when Elizabeth gave up Dudley, she offered him to Mary. It would have been a good political stroke, but surely there is something psychologically odd about it? Mary thought so, for she flew into a rage which shook the walls of Holyrood.

And finally, long after Mary had been executed by Elizabeth's command, Elizabeth herself lay dying. She wouldn't go to bed but lay on cushions day and night. Her bed would be her death-bed and she was not prepared to die. Did she feel she had not lived? Her one remaining duty was to name who should succeed her. And she, who had never failed her duty, couldn't bring herself to do it. At length Robert Cecil plucked up courage and whispered a name in her ear. She nodded, and died. The name was that of James Stuart, Mary Stuart's child.

It is all almost too felicitous dramatically, and I find it terribly moving as well.

To make one story of the two I had to adopt a form of play which could leap across both miles and months without a break, without a change of set; an overtly theatrical, highly artificial form. I happen to like that kind of play and no doubt was attracted to this subject by an intimation that some such form would be required.

I got so cavalier with miles and months at last that I put Mary and Elizabeth on stage together though the one remained in Scotland and the other in London. At Mary's crisis I brought Spain and Italy on stage as well and represented some months of critical diplomacy in a minute's interchange between the assembled potentates, presided over by John Knox with the Edinburgh mob as chorus in the wings. The stage at that juncture is no actual place, the minute that passes is not actual time; it is theatre merely.

By a more moderate distillation in the same convention I hoped to present the confused eventfulness of Mary's life as a series of single theatrical happenings, and to present the torturous complexities of Elizabeth's policy as an immediate response. I hoped, that is, that the two would pass a single narrative one to the other as relay runners exchange the baton. The point I am trying to make is this: that as a playwright I found the form exciting, and it was forced upon me by the historical facts.

I found the form exciting because I think that Theatre should be, not larger than life—I don't think anything can be that—but more significant than life, or rather—since nothing can be that either—should reveal the significance that is in life, proclaim that life does have significance.

There are plays I know, say Chekhov's, which drily demonstrate that life as we live it has little significance. But implicit in such plays is an invitation to live otherwise, an implication that we are letting life down. And there are plays (perhaps the best of our modern plays) which bitterly affirm that life *in its essence* has no significance. But the value of these plays is, as it seems to me, their bitterness. A Beckett character does not merely deny the existence of God he upbraids God (*le salaud*) for not existing. The implication is that God ought to exist, that life ought to have significance, is intolerable without it. And the start and conclusion of such plays is the existential determination to impose significance on life or penetrate life with significance, by an act of the human will.

Indeed, I can't see why a man who really believed (that is, believed and accepted) that life has and can have no significance should do anything at all, unless to end it. But write a play is the last thing he would do.

For there is something about Theatre—the framing of the action on the stage, the compression of the action in a little time, the bright lighting of the action, the knowledge of the audience that the action is predetermined (as it were artificially fated)—which compels the characters to be or seem significant. The most subtle analysis of life is perhaps to be found in the novel, the most lyric celebration of it perhaps in verse; but the giant exemplars of living (like Lear and Oedipus) are to be found on stage. It is no accident that Freud should name the springs of action after characters from Greek drama. And Shakespeare has the Prince of Denmark find himself inadequate by measurement against a Player King because the play's the thing which isolates and demonstrates whatever is significant in life. If nothing in life truly is significant then truly the best that Theatre can do is destroy itself and come to an end, in anti-theatre.

I am pro-Theatre. I do believe that even now life does somehow have some sort of significance. And if it is so then the need to say so was never more apparent. We have never made so poor a showing in our own eyes or the eyes of God or Nature. The Ten Commandments were never so regularly (or at least so effectively) broken as now. As a natural species we never till now threatened ourselves with extinction. And it seems to me that our poor showing is reciprocally the result and cause of our doubt of our significance. These youngsters taking drugs are not hedonists seeking merely pleasurable experience, they seek an experience so intensely pleasurable that it will seem significant. The Americans have long since realized that their war in Vietnam is senseless and continue to prosecute it with the cruelty of fanatics not because they are cruel but because they fear the awful blankness which will face them when they turn away from it. The student radical feels that he must set something on fire or kill or kidnap someone, not to solve a political problem but from a fundamentally noble anxiety to be serious. We are in some sort of psychic inflation, too much experience chasing too little emotion, and the value of experience is steadily debased. 'Sadistic!' 'Forbidden!' 'Shocking!' are no longer words from a pulpit to condemn the sadistic, forbidden and shocking. They are words outside a cinema meant hopefully to rouse enough half-hearted interest to take us inside. The drumskin has been battered slack, the strings of the instrument wrenched loose, we can no longer play a human tune; we have lost our significance.

Of course if we never had it then we have lost only an illusion and none of this matters. I am taking the view that all of it matters, that we did and do have significance, and that the Theatre is well-adapted to affirm it and not well-adapted to affirm anything else.

Certainly in life as we live it our significance is not readily apparent, and probably it never was. Most of what we say and do has no significance at all. Most of our time we merely pass.

Psychology to be sure tells us that all of what we say and do has deep significance, deepest when it seems most trivial because it is then that what we say and do, rightly interpreted, reveals unconscious impulse. And this is an interesting and useful insight. No modern playwright is unaware of it. It adds a little to the ways in which he can reveal significance. But only a little, for it is only rarely that an unconscious action is so eloquent that its significance is obvious. Freud likened the psyche to an ice-berg, nine-tenths of which is below the surface. Doubtless it is so; but we are not fish, to live below the surface. And psycho-analysis affords a very clumsy diving-bell; the light down there is uncertain. We live where we have always lived, up here in the air on this habitable tenth. And here most of our un-considered words and deeds are truly insignificant, or might as well be so since we are unaware of their significance.

It is only for a fraction of our lives, at moments of crisis, that we speak and act significantly and reveal or amend or damage our natures. Of course a crisis need not be a crisis of action. There are seemingly causeless inner crises, as we all know. And often enough such crises pass unnoticed by any but ourselves, perhaps because we have failed to meet them or else have met them and resolved them.

It indicates the nature of Theatre, what Theatre is good for and what not, that on the stage as not in life an inner crisis must have a cause which can be seen and issue in an adequate effect, or it will merely be bewildering. This is T. S. Eliot's famous 'objective correlation', the lack of which in *Hamlet*, the dis-proportion between Hamlet's gloom and his predicament, leads Eliot to judge *Hamlet* finally unsatisfactory. King Lear's inner crisis is quite clearly caused by his own wrongheaded action; and his inner crisis is so monumental that it can only issue adequately in his death. On stage that is. In life he might have ended comfortably in an old-folks' home. A modern playwright might well end *King Lear* so. And it would be an effectively cynical downbeat ending, revealing all that madness on the heath as so much flatulence and posturing. But paradoxically it would be an effective ending only in narrowly, almost academically theatrical terms, would only be effective because the audience, trained by Shakespeare, so confidently expected the other ending, the death. The author might be thought to have said something mocking about theatrical convention, but he would have said it only by leaning on that convention. He is at one remove further from life than Shakespeare because he is commenting on life only indirectly by commenting on

Shakespeare's treatment of it. If the audience had known throughout that the end of the play was an old-folks' home, that the madness was mere flatulence, the play throughout would be merely wearisome. Moreover this trick of crying 'Wolf!' and then producing a poodle, can only be played once or twice. My imaginary modern author is sawing through the branch on which he is sitting.

I have not seen *King Lear* so re-written, but I think I have seen it so directed. His dismembering of his kingdom was presented as an act of senile wilfulness (as indeed in real life it would have been), his subsequent madness (either as a necessary consequence of this or else deliberately) did indeed seem merely flatulent, and his final death no more than a pity. It was a most impressive piece of anti-theatre and I found it depressing. Destruction always is impressive, and depressing.

Now. If it is only for a fraction of our real lives that we speak and act significantly, that what we say and do expresses life's value, and if it is only that valuable element which I mean to put on stage, then I am to put people on stage as they are not in real life. And yet the audience must in some sense believe in them.

How am I to help my audience to this belief—or 'willing suspension of disbelief'? The obvious thing would seem to be to close the gap between the stage and life by having the stage imitate life as closely as possible. Beerbohm Tree put real live rabbits in Titania's wood. Alas, they stopped the show, which could not proceed until these furry atoms of real life had been chased from the stage; where they had no place. It was not merely that their authentic little presences underlined the artificiality of Titania's cardboard trees; they underlined the artificiality of the whole theatrical enterprise, the words and actions of the actors too. All professional actors know that they cannot compete on stage with an animal. This is not because animals are better actors; it is because they cannot act at all. Their helpless truthfulness to nature underlines the fact that the actor is 'only' acting. To invite direct comparison with life is theatrical suicide.

Of course the rabbits are a bit extreme, and Titania and the others were to speak not natural speech but Shakespearean speeches. If the setting were less ambitious (a contemporary drawing-room say instead of an Athenian wood) and the actors spoke less splendidly, might it not be possible to reproduce real life on stage? This is the 'fourth wall' drama, in which the proscenium arch is treated as a glass wall of the room where the actors are supposedly living out the action, unaware of the audience. Actors and set-designers of this school attain an extra-ordinary skill in reproducing the details of real life. But it remains a skill. The narrow limits of the stage continue to obtrude—those wings and drapes and changing lights are visible however cleverly disguised, those off-stage sound effects however like the real thing are obstinately sound-effects, off-stage; the comings and goings of the characters however nonchalantly executed remain entrances and exits ingeniously contrived by the dramatist so that the drama may unfold all in that one room. And if it is a drama, it is not the 'slice of life' which fourth wall drama aimed to be. If the play is to be a slice of life it must bear a one-to-one correlation to life, and the bulk of it must be undramatic. And an undramatic drama is nothing.

By dramatic I don't mean melodramatic. Chekhov is dramatic. But it is true that slice of life drama finds it more difficult to be dramatic than openly artificial drama. Playwrights of the school draw in their horns; instead of Kings and Princes in passionate conflict issuing in murders, they dealt in family misunderstand-ings issuing in an engagement or a bankruptcy. And actors of the school eschewed artificial eloquence of word and gesture and studied the stumblings of real life words and gestures. But stumblings which are studied are artificial stumblings, and latterly the most sincere and earnest actors of this school have brought genuine stumblings on stage, they have impro-vised, each night a new spontaneous performance sometimes with new words. This ought to give each night's performance a peculiar truth and freshness. But it doesn't. Wholehearted spontaneity is impossible on stage. Does the actor turn up at the theatre for each performance on spontaneous impulse every night? Is it his spontaneous wish each night to perform the part assigned to him and not another? Does he exit and enter as required by the other actors, spontaneously? It is a very compromised spontaneity. And compromised spontaneity is disagreeable. Personally, I find 'spontaneous' behaviour on the stage as uncomfortable as theatrical behaviour in real life. Both are false. Your rabbits are your only genuine improvisers.

The desire of these actors to be genuine is and historically was, a good reaction away from bombast, but the only way for an actor to be genuine is to accept that he is acting and be openly artificial. All these attempts to close the gap between the stage and real life by pretending that it isn't there are doomed, and widen it. The gap must be accepted and exploited by the actor and his audience and first and foremost by the playwright.

It is the inescapable artificiality of plays which makes the play form specially fit for the artificial distillation from real life of what seems to the playwright to be life's value. King Lear and Oedipus are valuable creations. They are figures of real significance. They embody truths about real life. But they are not as they would be in real life.

Now, for the playwright to accept the distance between theatre and life, the gap between the audience and the stage, is easier to talk about than do. He has a double loyalty, to actuality and to the theatre. He halves the difficulty if he puts his characters at an actual distance, a distance of time or a distance of place. Even Shakespeare never set a play in Elizabethan England. He set his people in the past or in some such never-never land as Venice or Illyria. Today when everyone has some idea what life is like in distant places, a distance of time is more effective. To show how an historical setting eases the playwright's problem, here are two great playwrights who show how hard the problem is when the setting is contemporary.

Ibsen's plays are monumental and tragic. But he wrote (mostly) of his contemporaries in a realistic style. And who in the audience does not feel uneasy as those prosaic figures in their raincoats and galoshes approach their tragic crises and threaten to burst into poetry? We half long for and half dread that they will do it. They must, or they will not be adequate to their predicaments. But if they do, we shan't believe them. And who in the audience does not feel an unworthy embarrassment, verging on hilarity, as the crisis of action arrives, off-stage (you cannot have an Oslo drawing-room littered with corpses like Elisinore)? As the Master Builder ascends his off-stage spire, the on-stage ladies wave and cheer and then (the author's stage directions) 'Suddenly there is a silence; the crowd utters a shriek of terror; a human body and some planks and poles can be indistinctly glimpsed falling through the trees'? (NB that prevaricating 'indistinctly'. Ibsen knew too much about audiences not to know that he was in some trouble with his audience here.) Or as Rosmer and Rebecca at the end of *Rosmersholm* go out to throw themselves in that thundering off-stage millrace 'through the hall' says the intrepid playwright 'and are seen to turn to the left'? Ibsen is so true to life, to the actual surface appearance of life, that we accept his characters as living people. If they go out to commit suicide we must either jump to our feet and protest, or remember that we are 'only' in the theatre. We are grateful when the curtain falls a few seconds later and we can applaud the heroic effort of the playwright and the actors to show us the ultimate in the ordinary.

Of the plays of Tennessee Williams the early *Glass Menagerie* is perfect. However, it is touching but not tragic, and the author moved on. For he too has the tragic sense of life. If he does not have the outrightly Jacobean sense of tragedy which Ibsen has he feels at any rate that life is tragically difficult. And this is not for him a philosophic judgement, he feels it urgently, here and now. It is actual life he must show on the

stage. And thereby show its tragic depths. Actual living is done
at the depths by three sorts of person, and tragedians have always
made use of them. They are saints, heroes and madmen. Looking
around at actual life Tennessee Williams saw no saints or heroes,
but madmen in plenty. Time was, you were not mad till you
were so mad that you had to be locked up. Since Freud the
distinction between madmen and ourselves has been less clear.
We see some method in their madness, much nonsense in our
rationality. Most of them are not locked up but out-patients,
merely 'Cases'. And from a Freudian standpoint we are all more
or less of a case, cunning out-patients as it were on the run. And
indeed the stress and tensions of life are such that there are
moments when we feel it is so, that to put back one's head and
howl would be a more appropriate (that is more sane) response
to life than our daily 'Good-Morning'. Obversely there are
moments when a well-behaved man, on his way to work say,
behaving as he is expected to behave, to the satisfaction of other
well-behaved men, looks at their faces and thinks to himself
'This is mad'. And though we later dismiss such moments as
aberrations we experienced them as moments of truth. So maybe
the mad are vessels of truth, and 'Cases' are test-cases for us all.
If so, by putting cases on the stage the playwright can put actual
life on stage in all authentic surface detail and yet reveal a deeper
truth about our superficially sane selves. And Tennessee Williams
puts them there with such delicate sympathy and fire that we
do respond to them. But not with cathartic terror and pity;
with pity only. We are not compelled to identify with them.
For they remain cases. The playwright has in a manner excused
the tragic depth of their predicament on the ground that they
are cases. On the same ground we excuse ourselves from full
participation in it. As Tennessee Williams wrote on he wrote of
cases more extreme. He did so not from a failure of taste or a
taste for the sensational. But since he had chosen the abnormal
to show the depths at the surface—outcrops of tragedy thrust
up through the plain of everyday appearance—so the deeper he

drove into tragedy the higher and more weirdly vertical his pinnacles of abnormality became. And when in *Night of the Iguana* an actor on stage describes at length and with obsessive eloquence a starving Indian peasant who picks out and swallows bits of undigested food from a hill of human excrement, it is no good having an actress turn up-stage to vomit on behalf of the audience. The audience has contracted out. The actor is not as we are if he can handle such muck with such fierce relish. And the actress is not as we are if her quick sympathy can leap clean over the immediate occasion and alight in India to share in that picking and swallowing so vividly that she must vomit. They are 'Cases'. The denouement of *Suddenly Last Summer* is so sadistic and bizarre that it verges on the hilarious, like those indistinctly falling planks and poles in the *Master Builder*. The trek of Tennessee Williams into the interior seems to me splendid; he could easily have shrunk from it and never crossed the limits of acceptable good taste. The fact remains that he showed abnormality to be a theatrical cul-de-sac.

Both he and Ibsen each allowed himself one play which so far from being trammelled in the familiar details of his own time and place is set at no time and place but is frankly fantastic. 'Reckless and formless' reported Ibsen gleefully of *Peer Gynt*. And as *Camino Real* got under way Tennessee Williams 'felt a new sensation of release'. Both plays are rarely produced, and rarely succeed in production. Both authors knew it would be so, or might be so. Then why did they so write? Here is the answer, from Tennessee Williams' foreword:

> More than any other work that I have done, this play has seemed to me like the construction of another world, a separate existence.

Is the man mad, does he think himself God to be constructing other worlds? No, but he is an artist and a bold one. All art as they say aspires to the condition of Music, which is the Queen of the Arts because it does not seek in any way to represent the real world, is not beholden to the real world but autonomous and need obey no laws but its own. When the clarinets come in on the flutes and the drums come in on both we may say 'I don't like it' but we can't say 'I don't believe it would happen in real life.' There is no question of it happening anywhere but in the concert hall. Not so with Theatre. What happens there must stand some comparison with what happens in real life. Yet Theatre is an art and does have laws of its own, which are not the laws of Nature. The other world which these two play-wrights in these two plays were trying to construct was only a world of Theatre, obeying its own laws. And if in these plays there is an element of self-indulgence, perhaps that is because both authors in the main body of their work have been over-conscientious in their fidelity to Nature, in allowing what is probable in life to dictate what is possible on stage.

And that fidelity is laudable. The humbler arts which lean on life have a dignity which the sovereign art of Music lacks. They are concerned. A man who is a musician may as a man be con-cerned. But Music is not. Theatre is. 'Of course,' says Tennessee Williams of that other world which he was trying to put on stage, 'it is nothing more nor less than my conception of the time and world I live in.'

The quotation is worth completing, for this is what he adds:

'And its people are mostly archetypes of certain basic attitudes and qualities.' If the play doesn't work, perhaps this is why. For people who are archetypes of attitudes and qualities aren't people. And if a play is to work properly its characters must be people, not archetypal but particular.

The problem then is how to trap them in particularity and yet release them from the details of the real world into a world that is theatrical.

One solution (not *the* solution but one solution) is to set them in a world as real as our own, but past. History is Dutch courage for the dramatist and for the audience both a pledge of actuality and a release from it. From men in cloaks and feathered hats we can accept a continuously high pitch of speech and action not because we seriously think they really did continuously speak and act like that but because we don't know how they spoke and only know the more dramatic of their actions. If I think of my next-door neighbour, I see a rumpled thing all blurred and merged into a wilderness of circumstances. If I think of Walter Raleigh I see a vivid figure floating free and capable of anything. It wasn't so of course. His life was just as bogged down in domestic detail as my neighbour's, and my own; but since my ignorance has freed him from domestic detail he will be as much at home on stage as any other place. The few things we do know of him are sufficiently dramatic in all conscience. And that's another thing.

The people that we know about from history tend to be important people, like Kings and Queens. Now I don't think that the life of a Queen is *ex-officio* any more significant, has any more value than the life of an ordinary person. Her actions have more consequences yes, but what consequences? Consequences, finally, for the lives of ordinary people. So the seeming significance which she derives from her office derives from the significance of ordinary people, and can't be more. Whatever significance she has, she has as a woman. She may be a great woman, a great soul with more significance than most of us, but she might have been that in any station. A woman dying old and lonely is just that. It does not alter her predicament that she is splendidly dressed and may give orders and be obeyed.

But it does throw her predicament—the predicament of any such old woman—into theatrical relief. She who plays the Queen may enter from nowhere along a red carpet to a fanfare of trumpets and express her predicament in speech of such magnificence and accuracy as no real woman ever spoke, yet cause the audience no discomfort. She who plays the wife of a suburban grocer must come in from the bus-stop, hang up her raincoat, and express herself as eloquently as is plausible. Small wonder that so many realistic plays have centred on our failure to communicate. The fanfare and the carpet are theatrical devices, with an historical excuse.

Shakespeare's people spoke blank verse, which no real people ever did, in ancient Rome no more than in Elizabethan London. It is the language of Theatre only. He sets his play in Rome not London to avoid an irrelevant comparison between his speeches and real speech. He wants his unreal speech to be accepted.

And he wants it accepted in all its unreality, as actual theatre not imitation life. He underlines its unreality by slipping in colloquial scenes replete with Elizabethan slang. He emphasizes that the actor is not really Julius Caesar by giving him a chiming clock; Macbeth's Porter comments on Elizabethan politics; Lear's Fool on Tudor local government; deliberate anachronisms to remind his audience that the gap between themselves and the characters is not historical but theatrical. To keep his audience he must still provide good theatre; but it will be good or bad by theatre's laws, not the laws of ancient Rome.

Why set it then in ancient Rome? Because it must be set somewhere, somewhere concrete. And it is only very rarely that even the very greatest playwrights succeed in making concrete the country of the mind. (I think Shakespeare does it in *The Tempest* and Samuel Beckett in *Waiting For Godot*.) And Shakespeare and his audiences venerated ancient Rome. It made good matter for Elizabethan theatre. For all their vivid individuality Caesar's assassins in Shakespeare's play go about it gravely aware of their historical importance, knowing that it is ordained, a ritual almost—as Theatre was in its beginning. 'Bear it,' Brutus tells the others, 'as our Roman actors do, with untired spirits and formal constancy.' He meant Elizabethan London actors of course.

An interest in the past and an interest in the present are not mutually exclusive; indeed you cannot understand either, without some understanding of both for they are not discontinuous. I wrote a play about Sir Thomas More and in America it was thought relevant to Senator McCarthy's persecution of the Left.

And though Shakespeare never set a play in Elizabethan London yet Elizabethan London breathes in Shakespeare's plays. He clearly relished the life of his own time and had a decent concern for contemporary issues. But he was a man of the Theatre heart and soul, and dealt with contemporary issues at the proper theatrical distance.

Despite which, and to conclude, I have to confess a less worthy reason for writing historical plays. I would claim, like Shakespeare, to be concerned for my own times. But I am not sure that I relish them. 'Things fall apart; the centre cannot hold.' Indeed they do; I fear it can't. And I don't like it. And have a love of old things, old buildings, books, pictures and music, which I suspect is reprehensible. Are they really, as they seem to me, more human than our own new things, or older merely? There is no going back to them in any case. And now I come to think of that, I realize I wouldn't want to. I belong then to the present. Good. I wish the present were more human though, that people were not so distressed, and things were made with more respect.

ROBERT BOLT

February 1971

A NOTE TO THE DESIGNER

I have tried to assume enough for you to work upon yet not so much as to prevent your making a substantial contribution to the style of production.

You will see that the stage serves at one moment for the Court of England and at the next for the Court of Scotland. I hope the properties will be solid and pleasurable in themselves to look at, but that the lighting, not the properties, will create the changes of time and place and mood. I hope the costumes will convey the extravagances and extremes of the period, yet not distract the audience nor tie up the actors.

I have assumed: one, a flat-topped pyramid or flight of shallow steps, supporting a screen or curtain in the First Act and the throne in the Second Act; two, a table with stools; three, a 'pulpit' though this could be a mere lectern; four, a hanging or revolving cloth of State. My intention is to maintain a smoothly continuous narrative to which changes of time and place will seem incidental.

PRINCIPAL CHARACTERS IN ORDER OF THEIR APPEARANCE

LADIES: Pretty, flighty, privileged, young.

NAU: An elderly bachelor; gentle, learned, anxious, utterly upright, deeply affectionate.

MARY: Overbred, refined and passionate; sympathetic, beautiful, intelligent and brave. But sensual and subjective. Born a Queen, deferred to from the cradle, it is a tribute to her nature that she is not simply spoiled. But she mistakes her public office for a private attribute.

CECIL: A top flight Civil Servant, reasonable, courteous, ruthless.

ELIZABETH: Personable, wilful, highly-strung. But schooled to clear sight and tuned to self-discipline by a dangerous and lonely childhood. Commencing her reign as a natural perhaps just faintly neurotic young woman, her strength of character is such that she meets the unnatural demands of Queenship with increasing brilliance, in an increasing rage of undisclosed resentment.

DUDLEY: A tall, hard, virile animal; unintellectual but nobody's fool.

KNOX: A pedant and a demagogue, a nasty combination. But palpably, frighteningly sincere.

MORTON: Renaissance noble and tribal Chief; seasoned and at ease in every kind of villainy.

RIZZIO: A likeable hedonist, affectionate and sceptical; but a lightweight; precarious.

BOTHWELL: Shrewd, coarse-natured, irresponsible; but uncomplaining as unpitying, genuinely a law unto himself; a dangerous vortex to dependent natures.

BISHOP: A conscientious career clergyman, a bit selfish, a bit ignoble; but he knows that.

WALSINGHAM: A Puritan and humourless on principle, but dangerously intelligent; a selfless intriguer, a dedicated wolf.

DE QUADRA: Walsingham's opposite, suave in manner; equally dedicated, equally dangerous.

DARNLEY: A tall, athletic, good looking aristocrat; too young, too merely pleasant to withstand the heavy personal and public pressures bearing on him.

ORMISTON: A ragged Border ruffian. Middle-aged, his moral sense quite atrophied.

DAVISON: A slightly built youth of good family. Too generous by nature for the trade of politics.

PRISONER: A scholar priest worn thin by the life of a secret agent.

SCOTS LAIRDS, SERVANTS, CLERKS.

CAST OF FIRST PERFORMANCE

Vivat! Vivat Regina! was first presented at the Chichester Festival Theatre, on
20 May 1970, with the following cast:

CATHERINE DE MEDICI	Mairhi Russell
MARY, QUEEN OF SCOTS	Sarah Miles
FRANCOIS II, KING OF FRANCE	Michael Feast
THE CARDINAL OF LORRAINE	William Hutt
ELIZABETH I OF ENGLAND	Eileen Atkins
WILLIAM CECIL	Richard Pearson
ROBERT DUDLEY	Norman Eshley
JOHN KNOX	Leonard Maguire
BAGPIPER	Willie Cochrane
LORD MORTON	Archie Duncan
DAVID RIZZIO	Barry Jackson
LORD BOTHWELL	David McKail
CLAUD NAU	Charles Lloyd Pack
A BISHOP	Brian Hawksley
A CLERIC	Robin Humphreys
SIR FRANCIS WALSINGHAM	Edgar Wreford
DE QUADRA	Edward Atienza
A MESSENGER	Michael Feast
HENRY STUART, LORD DARNLEY	James Warwick
LORD MOR	Cyril Wheeler
A DOCTOR	Roger Rowland
TALA	Charles Houston
ORMISTON	Jonathan Mallard
DAVISON	Philip Anthony
EARL OF SHREWSBURY	Brian Hawksley
A PRISONER	Charles Houston
FRANCIS, DUKE OF ALENCON	Milo Sperber
RUTHVEN	Leon Greene
LINDSAY	Thick Wilson
FALCONSIDE	Raymond Skipp
KERR	Antony Milner
DOUGLAS	Jonathan Mallard
AN ARCHBISHOP	Kenneth McClellan
PHILIP, KING OF SPAIN	Antony Milner
THE POPE	Robert Selbie
A PRIEST	John Herrington
JAILERS	David Gwillim: Raymond Skipp
BREWER	David Gwillim
COURTIERS, LAIRDS, CLERKS, SERVANTS	David Gwillim: John Herrington: Carolyn Lyster: Melinda May: John O'Brien: Mary Savage: Raymond Skipp: Cyril Wheeler

The Play was Directed by PETER DEWS
Designed by CARL TOMS
Music Composed and Arranged by RICHARD KAYNE

The Chichester Festival Production of *Vivat! Vivat Regina!* in the revised text, as published here, was presented by H. M. Tennent Ltd. and John Clements Plays Ltd at the Piccadilly Theatre, London, on 8 October 1970, with the following cast:

MARY, QUEEN OF SCOTS	Sarah Miles
CLAUD NAU	David Bird
WILLIAM CECIL	Richard Pearson
ELIZABETH I OF ENGLAND	Eileen Atkins
ROBERT DUDLEY	Norman Eshley
JOHN KNOX	Leonard Maguire
BAGPIPER	Willie Cochrane
DAVID RIZZIO	Matthew Guinness
LORD MORTON	Archie Duncan
LORD BOTHWELL	David McKail
LORD BISHOP OF DURHAM	Brian Hawksley
A CLERIC	Kenneth Caswell
SIR FRANCIS WALSINGHAM	Edgar Wreford
DE QUADRA	Edward Atienza
DAVISON	Eilian Wyn
HENRY STUART, LORD DARNLEY	Cavan Kendall
LORD MOR	Brian Hawksley
RUTHVEN	Glyn Grain
LINDSEY	Alexander John
A DOCTOR	Ken Grant
TALA	Malcolm Rogers
ORMISTON	Jonathan Mallard
A PRISONER	Malcolm Rogers
SCOTS ARCHBISHOP	Maurice Jones
PHILIP, KING OF SPAIN	Alastair Meldrum
THE POPE	Kenneth Caswell
JAILERS	Adrian Reynolds: Ken Grant
BREWER	Adrian Reynolds
COURTIERS, LAIRDS, CLERKS, SERVANTS	Glyn Grain: Ken Grant: Maurice Jones: Alastair Meldrum: Adrian Reynolds
COURT LADIES	Isabel Metliss: Angela Easton

The Play was Directed by PETER DEWS
Designed by CARL TOMS
Lighting by MICK HUGHES
Music Composed and Arranged by RICHARD KAYNE

Vivat! Vivat
Regina!

ACT ONE

Exterior. Dappled sunlight on leaves and fruit. Enter two LADIES, NAU *following. They cross to seat, where* LADIES *turn and regard him with impudent curiosity over their fans.*

1ST LADY: If you wait here sir, the Queen will pass.
NAU: Thank you.
1ST LADY: We'll wait with you.
> *They sit. He, between a smile and irritation.*
NAU: Do I look as though I mean her any mischief?
2ND LADY: In my experience old gentlemen mean mischief most when they least look it sir.
NAU: I'm sorry your experience has been of such a nature.
> *He leaves them. They look after him blankly. Look at one another, shrug.*
2ND LADY: A heavy fellow, whoever he may be. Go on.
> *They gossip.*
1ST LADY: Well—It seems poor Chloe got the Cardinal to bed at last, but he could not perform—
2ND LADY: The Cardinal—?
1ST LADY: Could not perform at all, though he laboured like a windmill—(*Breaks off as* NAU *turns.*)—What sir, do I shock you?
NAU: No. But you disgrace yourself.
2ND LADY: He is a priest.
NAU: Are only priests respectable?
1ST LADY: That's true; he is respectable, he cannot be a priest. At length it seems she lumbers out of bed, quite naked—
2ND LADY: Oh Lord, Chloe, naked.
1ST LADY: It confounds imagination does it not—?—And says

—(*Giggles.*) 'If this is all Y'r'Em'nance can do, what brings Y'r Em'nance to my bed?' And His Em'nance answers 'Spiritual Pride my child; it's Lent, and you were one of my austerities.'

They laugh. NAU *looking at them thoughtfully.*

Oh come sir, surely you can smile to hear a mucky tale?

NAU: Not hearing it from one who waits upon the Queen.

1ST LADY: Why, don't you think the Queen would smile?

NAU: You would not tell her such a tale?

1ST LADY: I see you do not know the Queen.

NAU (*uneasy*): I do begin to doubt I do.

2ND LADY: I doubt you ever did.

NAU: I was her teacher, Madam.

1ST LADY: Oh. Well if you were sir she has made a good recovery. (*Looks off.*) I'll tell my tale, and she will smile.

They rise as CHAMBERLAIN *enters.*

CHAMBERLAIN: Ho there—the Queen!

NAU *withdraws and watches attentively as* MARY *enters to fanfare, bestows a brief good morning smile on the* LADIES *who curtsey and kiss her hands.*

MARY: Ladies.

She drifts past them.

2ND LADY: Your Grace, Mathilde has a marvellous mucky tale to tell.

MARY (*faint smile*): It would be marvellous if Mathilde had not.

1ST LADY: Oh.

MARY (*half apologetic*): I am not in the mucky mood, Mathilde. (*Turning towards them.*) I am looking for an old, white-headed gentleman—

1ST LADY: —This gentleman?

NAU: Mignon.

He is beaming but she stops and awkwardly turns away:

MARY: You have ridden hard, Claud. I heard you were no further on than Paris, yesterday.

NAU: I rode all night.

MARY: Why?

NAU: Why Mignon, to be here with you.

MARY: I was your Mignon, when I was your pupil, sir.

She turns and he, bewildered, drops to one knee.

NAU: Your Grace.

The LADIES *too are surprised by her behaviour.*

MARY: Leave us, ladies.

They curtsey and go. MARY *crosses, offers hand, formal.*

Well travelled Claud from Scotland, and well returned to
France.

NAU: Your Grace.

He kisses hand, rises and watches as she walks away.

MARY: Upon what care of state I wonder has my mother
sent you back. I'm sure it is some care of state, no care for
me.

NAU: Before all else I am to tell you that your mother loves you
well Your Grace.

MARY: My mother does not know me, sir.

NAU: That is her sorrow too. The ruling of your Scottish
kingdom in your name has kept your mother from you. And
that is love and not the lack of it.

MARY: A kind of love.

NAU: The hardest kind.

MARY: Aye. And granite too is hard. But I have yet to hear it
is a good material to make a cradle of. I tell you sir, no care
of state should keep me from my child . . . Come, let me
know your charges.

NAU: Your Grace has in a manner touched upon my first.
Your Grace, your mother wonders if Your Grace may
presently, in probability, expect a child.

MARY: She wonders that?

NAU: Your Grace.

MARY: I wonder much that she should wonder that. I wonder
you should ask . . . Have you not waited on my husband,
Claud?

NAU: But now, Your Grace.

MARY: Did you not see his face? They sometimes draw the curtains, to spare his visitors his face.

NAU: I saw, Your Grace.

MARY: And having seen his face—And having seen the suppurating sores that batten on his poor young mouth—and having seen his ancient eyes—sir, do you ask—do you of all men dare to ask if presently in probability I may expect a child?

NAU (*kneeling*): Pardon.

MARY: No! You shall not have my pardon now . . .

But seeing the pathetic kneeling figure on a sudden note of lament and reproach:

Oh Claud, I was a little girl; and you were all the father and the mother that I had; you taught me how to read and write; and when I got my lessons well—Good God you sat me on your knee and said I was your best of little girls! And when I got my lessons ill my sharpest punishment was your displeasure! . . . And you stood by and said no word and let them marry me to syphilis! No—!—You shall not have my pardon now!

NAU: My word carried no weight Your Grace—Beseech Your Grace, believe I spoke!

MARY: You spoke no word to me.

NAU: They said it would be Treason and the axe if I should speak that word to you. They stopped my mouth with fear— Nay with my own cowardice.

MARY: Oh . . .Oh.

She crosses; raises him.

I'm glad that it was cowardice. Connivance I could not have pardoned.

NAU: And am I truly pardoned now?

MARY: Truly and gladly. I wept in puddles when you went away to Scotland, Claud.

NAU: I too.

MARY: You wept?

NAU: I wept with due decorum but, oh yes, I wept.

MARY (*smiling*): 'With due decorum'. Oh welcome back . . . It was my mother offered you the axe if you should tell me, was it not?

NAU: It was.

MARY: For love of me?

NAU: She made the match for love of you. Your husband is the King of France. You are the Queen of Scots. And France and Scotland joined might get your English Kingdom too.

MARY: Would you, for fifty Englands, kiss my husband on the mouth?

He cannot meet her eyes. Looks after her as she leaves him.

NAU: Can they not cure him, Madam?

MARY: If prayer and care can cure him, I will do it. I do not think the doctors can.

NAU: God Bless Your Grace.

MARY: Aye, bless me, Claud, I also pray for him to die.

NAU: Mignon!

MARY: Yes. And for myself to have a husband I might love.

NAU: Nay now, you must love the one you have.

MARY: I am forbid to touch him, Claud.

NAU: There is a love that needs no touching.

MARY: With such a love as that I love him. But what kind of 'love' is that?

NAU: The royal kind. The King of Heaven loves us all with such a love as that.

MARY: I know it sir. (*Crosses herself.*) And holy nuns return his love; but then they are betrothed to Christ. My husband was betrothed to death upon the day that he was born. And I have no such high vocation as a nun.

NAU (*stern*): You ought to have; you have high office.

MARY: I know that too, sir. (*Leaving him.*) Right well I know. (*She is abstracted.*) . . . What is your second charge?

NAU: Nay let us finish with the first—(*Severe.*) Mignon, do you mean to take a lover?

MARY: . . . I mean to hear your second charge.

NAU: The treaty which your mother has negotiated with the English.

Indifferent, her thoughts elsewhere—

MARY: Well?

NAU: The English have desired another term.

MARY: Oh?

NAU: Your Grace shows here (*he indicates the cloth of state*) the lion of Scotland and the English leopard.

She begins to pay attention.

MARY: Yes?

NAU: The English now desire you to take down the leopard and show the lion only.

MARY: No.

NAU: Your Grace it is the express desire of the English Queen.

MARY: Of whom?

NAU: Your Grace she is effectively the Queen.

MARY: Elizabeth fitz Tudor is a bastard and a heretic and cannot be a Queen.

NAU: She sits on a throne.

MARY: A dog can do that. No, I will not sign this treaty, Claud.

NAU: Then the English army will remain in Scotland, where it lives right barbarously on the common people.

MARY: You are clever, Claud.

NAU: Your Grace I hope is pitiful.

MARY: Let her be pitiful—It is her army!

NAU: They are your people.

MARY (*shrugs*): Well I will sign it. And she is Queen indeed.

NAU: In this you show more Queen than she.

MARY: Aye anything that makes me less makes me more Queen, Claud, does it not?

NAU: There is much truth in that.

MARY: There is no truth at all in that. And I am sick of hearing that. Diminish me, the Queen's diminished. Starve me and the Queen will fail. If I am sickly, she is pale. I am the Queen and more the Queen the *more* I am myself!

It is a credo, passionate. He looks at her thoughtfully and then:

NAU: So thinks Elizabeth.

MARY (*sour indifference*): Indeed.

NAU: Indeed. She too mistakes her office for herself. And thinks that her whole duty is to do as she desires.

MARY: She has not had the advantage of your ceaseless moralizing, Claud.

NAU: Perhaps that's it. For she will have what she desires and it will fetch her off the throne.

MARY (*startled*): What—?—Why what does she desire?

NAU: A husband she might love.

MARY: What husband?

NAU: Her lover.

MARY (*incredulous*): Robert Dudley?

NAU: She loves him.

MARY: But he's a Commoner.

NAU: She loves him for himself, perhaps.

MARY: He has a wife.

NAU: He does not love his wife.

MARY: So?

NAU (*suddenly stern, heavy with distaste*): So his wife must die.

MARY: . . . How, die?

NAU: Violently.

MARY: Are they mad?

NAU: They see no duty but their duty to themselves. And that is mad.

MARY: Oh let them do it . . . Let them do it!

NAU: Can you rejoice at murder?

MARY: Nay Claud, you said yourself this thing will fetch her off the throne.

NAU: Then Queen then must rejoice. I had thought *yourself* more natural.

MARY: You are my teacher still . . . But is it true?

NAU: Your mother thinks it true.

MARY: I'll warrant she rejoices at it. (*Then seeing something in his face:*) What is it, Claud?

NAU: Your mother does not much rejoice at anything, Your Grace.

MARY: Why?

NAU: Your Grace, she is dying.

MARY: Oh.

> *She moves, checks, sharply:*

You should have told me this at first.

NAU: I was instructed to retain it till the last.

MARY: Why?

NAU: Your royal mother charged me thus: She said: 'Our daughter must think first upon these high affairs of state, not discomposed by any grief she may be pleased to feel, upon our dying.'

> *She stares at him. Softly:*

MARY: She said that?

NAU: Your Grace.

MARY (*almost whispering*): Dying, she said *that*?

NAU: Your Grace.

MARY: Oh Claud—I would to God that I had known her!

> *Her face crumples, streaming with silent tears she raises and lets fall her arms in a gesture of utter helplessness, and goes, blindly. He looks after her.*

NAU: Oh too much passion, too much.

> *He collects himself, going quickly after her, calls formal:*

Ho there—The Queen!

> *Fanfare. He exits. Light change to cold interior as leaves and flowers fly out.* SERVANTS *enter, place table and throne.* CECIL *enters.*

CECIL: Ho there the Queen!

> *Fanfare.* ELIZABETH *makes a royal entrance.* SERVANTS *bow and Exit as she sits.*

CECIL: Your Grace, even a sovereign cannot do what is impossible.

ELIZABETH: For me to marry Robert Dudley is not impossible.

CECIL: For Your Grace to marry him and remain Queen of England is impossible. (*Gentle insistence.*) He must to prison.

ELIZABETH: We do not know yet that he did it!

CECIL: It would appear that he did it. That being so it must be made apparent that Your Grace did not. Your Grace must think how such a marriage would be taken in France and Spain, as well as here at home.

ELIZABETH: Must I marry to please France and Spain?

CECIL: Your Grace, this marriage would delight them. When Mary Stuart heard of it she cried out: 'Let them do it!'

ELIZABETH: She said that?

CECIL: That and more Your Grace.

ELIZABETH: What more?

CECIL: Such stuff as I cannot repeat to Your Grace.

ELIZABETH: She is free in her ways, that Mary.

CECIL: She can afford to be Your Grace. She is Queen of France, and France is rich. She is Queen of Scots, and Scotland is the rear gate to England. The Catholic half of England thinks that she is Queen of England too . . . And she cried out 'Let them do it!'

ELIZABETH: Well; I would not delight Mary by my marriage. Nor will I not marry to displease her! I will marry as my heart and conscience say.

CECIL: Conscience . . .! In Spain they are saying openly: 'What kind of a State Church is this, where the Head of the State, the Head of the Church, will not only let a man murder his wife—but marry him for't?' . . . Your Grace, he must to prison.

ELIZABETH: But what if he is innocent?

CECIL: He must to prison pending an enquiry which will find him innocent.

ELIZABETH: Call him. (CECIL *going*.) William. (*He stops.*) What if he is guilty?

CECIL: In that case too he must to prison pending an enquiry, which will find him innocent. In neither case can Your Grace marry him.

ELIZABETH: Call him.

CECIL: Be wise Your Grace.

ELIZABETH: As wise as I can. (*And as he still hesitates, angrily:*) I cannot be wiser!

CECIL (*calls*): Robert Dudley.

> DUDLEY *strides in carrying his rapier and belt. He chucks this down, glances at* CECIL, *stands bristling before* ELIZABETH, *goes down on one knee. For a moment their glances lock; then she looks away and:*

ELIZABETH: Well sir, rise, and tell it.

> *He rises, flashes a resentful look at* CECIL *and sneers:*

DUDLEY: Haven't you been told?

ELIZABETH: Not by you.

DUDLEY: No—*I* have been kept outside your door! Three days! Three nights!

ELIZABETH: Tell it.

DUDLEY: There was a fair at Abingdon. She didn't go herself. But she sent all her servants.

CECIL: So she was alone.

DUDLEY: I didn't know she was alone; I was in London.

CECIL: Why all her servants—Was she so kind?

DUDLEY: . . . Yes.

ELIZABETH: I never heard you say so.

DUDLEY: . . . No.

CECIL: Well sir.

DUDLEY: They came back in the evening. And found her. On the floor of the hall. Below the stairs.

CECIL: With her neck broken.

DUDLEY: I was in London.

CECIL: And, your agents?

DUDLEY: What 'agents'?

CECIL: Oh come sir.

DUDLEY: I didn't *hear* of it until that night!

CECIL: How did you hear of it?

DUDLEY: How? . . . God forgive me, right gladly.

ELIZABETH: Oh Robin.

DUDLEY: And you?

ELIZABETH: God pity me, right gladly too.

CECIL: These past six months sir, you have put it around that your wife was sick and like to die.

DUDLEY: Yes.

CECIL: And was she?

DUDLEY: No.

CECIL: These stairs now—

DUDLEY: Elmwood. Polished.

CECIL: Ah, polished. She slipped then.

DUDLEY: I suppose so.

CECIL: It was an accident; she fell, from the stairs.

DUDLEY: I suppose so.

ELIZABETH: Robin she was lying fifteen feet from the stairs— She was thrown!

DUDLEY: . . . Yes! Yes. She was thrown! No not by me. Or by my agency. She threw herself.

ELIZABETH: Herself . . . But why?

DUDLEY: Because she *knew* that I would hear of it—right gladly.

ELIZABETH: Oh God . . .

DUDLEY: I put it around that she was sick and like to die because I hoped—God damn me black, I hoped that one who loved me or desired my favour might . . . do it. Well now. One who loved me and desired my favour, *has*.

ELIZABETH: . . . Oh Robin, either this is true or else you are a devil.

DUDLEY: You must decide that Madam, I've done.

ELIZABETH: But can there be such love? Robin, I would not do that for you.

DUDLEY: Well love is never equal. I would for you.

ELIZABETH: Sir, I think this gentleman is innocent.

CECIL is unresponsive.

Well, speak.

CECIL: Am I to say what I think Your Grace, or what you want to hear?

ELIZABETH: Oh Cecil, can they never be the same?

CECIL (*shrugs*): Then I say, with Mary Stuart: 'Let them do it'.

DUDLEY: What's this?

CECIL: Sir the Queen believes you innocent—and I am ready to believe you innocent—but the Queen, alas, is not the country, nor am I—And you must understand—

DUDLEY: I understand no word you say. Can't you speak like a man?

CECIL: To speak like a 'man' sir—If the Queen takes you to bed she will lie down Elizabeth the First and rise the second Mrs Dudley.

DUDLEY: . . . *Zounds!*—

He lunges for his sword.

ELIZABETH: Put that up!

She gets up, goes and stands below the cloth of state.

You may withdraw.

DUDLEY: I?

ELIZABETH: Yes Robin.

DUDLEY: And he stays?

ELIZABETH: Yes Robin.

He stares one moment. Snatches up his rapier, says to CECIL:

DUDLEY: Cecil, you have ruined me, and I will not forget it.

CECIL: You are wrong sir, I have saved you. And belike I have made your fortune. And you will forget it.

DUDLEY snatches a bow at ELIZABETH, *goes.*

ELIZABETH: Cecil, were the summers better than they are now, when you were a child?

CECIL: Your Grace—? . . . Yes Your Grace, I share that common illusion. The summers then were nothing but sunshine. I and the weather have declined together.

ELIZABETH: Who raised you, Cecil?

CECIL: My father and my mother, Madam.

ELIZABETH: It is not sunshine you remember; it is love. My father killed my mother and disowned me, and I can't remember a summer when it was not raining after that. I was raised by cautious strangers in the shadows, between prisons. I was taught: Mathematics, Latin, Greek, and caution, too well; and saw too soon where love could lead. Prisons were familiar, and so I put my heart into protective custody. But Cecil I mislaid the key, and it has lain in darkness, cold and calcifying these twenty years. And Cecil, Robin had a magic word, which opened doors for me . . . You said that you would be my servant and my friend, and will you be my jailer?

CECIL *is moved, but:*

CECIL: Something of each Your Grace. Your Grace's Councillor.

ELIZABETH *looks at him.*

ELIZABETH: Aye. Well then. To Council.

CECIL: And . . . the gentleman?

ELIZABETH: To prison. (*Going.*)

CECIL: Your Grace.

She hears the discreet satisfaction in his voice and turns.

ELIZABETH: But Cecil, we believe him innocent. And if from now until your dying day, you whisper one word to the contrary; we will punish you.

Light change. Thunder. Enter KNOX *in a dripping cloak; he shakes it, water falling in a puddle at his feet. Looks up and:*

KNOX: Welcome to Scotland. And welcome to St Andrew's Kirk, but lately called 'Cathedral'—for it isnae long since a great fat 'bishop', in 'vestments'—like a prostitute in her undergarments—was wont to jabber forth the Word of God in heathen Latin from that very pulpit—Tchah!

*He crosses to the pulpit, flips down the cross, flips up the drape, is
about to continue his address, checks, sniffs and:*
D'you know what I smell here? Scent. (*Sniffs again at the pulpit.*)
Aye, perfume. (*Looks round.*) The whole place needs scrubbin'!
It still reeks of Catholicism!
Controls himself. Walks away.
Well well, yon fat lad'll no enjoy his 'tithes' where he is now.
We hastened him where he come from (*jabbing downwards*) wi'
a length of rope. And you'll look hard for a Catholic priest in
Scotland now. Scotsmen can stand upright! We have a godly
governance . . .! Or did until today. Today it seems once more
we have a Queen amongst us. And that's my matter.
Crosses briskly to pulpit and mounts.
Beloved brethren. Certain of the Ancient Fathers make a
question of it whether women have immortal souls like men
or else like animals are morsels of mere Nature.
Breaks off, leans forward, confidential:
Er, this is my First Blast of the Trumpet Against the Monstrous
Regiment of Women. Yes, I John Knox that am the Father
of the Kirk and spake with Calvin as a friend, regard myself
as naething mair than a wee trumpet in the hands of the
Almighty . . . And if that's not humility, I'd like to know
what is . . .
He resumes his formal academic manner.
Now. If the Fathers make a question of it, then it is in doubt.
Doubt is a lesser thing than certainty. It is a certainty that men
have souls. So: Woman is a lesser thing than man.
Leans forward, impressively:
That being so, the Regiment of women *over* men is monstrous
—And we must take it as a visitation and a punishment—as
was proved upon us lately by that tiger Mary Guise, as proves
upon the English by that wolf Elizabeth, and as will prove
upon us once again by that she cat Mary Stuart, now unhappily
amongst us following the death—the *mysterious* death—of her
wee French husband. No more of that. They that have ears,

let them hear. He was they say, unable to supply her raging appetite.

Light change, exterior. KNOX *sits, disappearing. Enter* BAG-PIPER, *playing, followed by* MARY, *wearing crimson. She sits. She is followed by* LADIES, RIZZIO *and* NAU, *all in grey silk aflutter with white favours. Last come the* SCOTS LORDS *wearing black faintly relieved by sombre plaids. The entourage groups itself about* MARY. *The* SCOTS LORDS *stand in a stiff line behind the solemn* BAGPIPER *who plays on.*

MARY *and entourage have difficulty in suppressing their amusement. Seeing this,* MORTON *steps forward from among the* LORDS *and jabs* BAGPIPER *in the ribs. Startled, he stops and his instrument falls silent with a long-drawn melancholy wail.*

MARY *registers the stone-faced* LORDS.

MARY: My lords, forgive us. Our ear is not yet tuned to this wild instrument.

MORTON: Certainly Madam, it is no lute.

RIZZIO *picks out a mocking little chord on the strings of his beribboned instrument and* MARY *sharply:*

MARY: Davie—have done . . . Where is Lord Bothwell?

BOTHWELL (*steps forward*): Madam.

MARY: Here sir.

She goes and gives him a purse.

MARY: We thank you for conducting us from France in safety, through such storms.

BOTHWELL (*looking up at her*): Were there storms, Madam—?— I didn't notice.

MARY: Ah—A Scot can turn a compliment!

BOTHWELL: Aye—given a strong stimulus.

MARY: Will you remain in Edinburgh?

BOTHWELL: I am the Lord Lieutenant of the *Border*, Madam.

She sits again, straight-backed and formal.

MARY: They tell me you steal sheep across the Border, Bothwell.

BOTHWELL: Aye, Madam, English sheep.

MARY: We would not have our cousin Elizabeth provoked.

BOTHWELL: Oh they're not her sheep. They're Harry Percy's.

MARY: Lord Bothwell, we have come here to rule.

BOTHWELL: And welcome to Your Grace's bonny face.

He goes out.

MARY: Morton, this Border raiding must be stopped.

MORTON: It can't be stopped Your Grace. Lord Bothwell is the head of the Clan Hepburn.

MARY: So?

MORTON: The Border is Hepburn country.

MARY: All Scotland is my country, my lord.

MORTON: But Your Grace has no men.

MARY: But haven't you—my Lords in Council—men?

MORTON: Aye, Madam. *We* have.

MARY: Well, no doubt we will atune ourselves to both your music and your manners. Now, we will to supper.

MORTON: Now we must to Kirk, Madam.

MARY: 'Must' we?

NAU (*quick confidential warning*): Yes.

MARY (*swallows her anger, shrugs*): Well then, to Kirk.

She rises. Light change, church interior. RIZZIO *and* NAU *move chair.* LORDS *and* ENTOURAGE *counter-march. Fall still all looking upwards at the pulpit on which the lights come up again.*

KNOX: You may read in Revelations of a Great Whore; dressed in scarlet; sitting on a throne.

A stir among the ENTOURAGE *they look at* MARY.

MARY: If I had known your text good Master Knox I would have worn a different garment.

KNOX: Nae doubt.

MARY: Now that you have seen my garment, no doubt you will change your text.

KNOX: I have nae mind to.

RIZZIO: Then you insult the Queen.

KNOX: Signor Rizzio, they tell me you're Her Grace's favourite musician. What more ye may be to Her Grace, God knows.

You're not a theologean. The Great Whore in the Book of
Revelations is no Queen—though Queens may be great
whores—she is the Church of Rome!

MARY: Now prove that Master Knox or by Heaven I will have
God's Trumpet scoured—for I find it something dirty.

KNOX: Prove it quotha! Secret murders and strange painted
vices, whispering together in the shadows of the Vatican is
thought by some sufficient proof.

   Murmur of approval from the LORDS.

Screeching choirs of castratos and great bronze bells to drown
the outcries of the poor is thought by some sufficient proof!

   A loud murmur from the LORDS. *He is intoxicated.*

Elaborate, blasphemous, tinkling show in place of sober piety
is thought by some—Aye Madam you may laugh!

MARY: Marry I must. I have heard this vulgar stuff a hundred
times before and know how to refute it.

KNOX: Do so.

MARY: Shall I?

RIZZIO: —Briefly.

MARY: Suppose the Holy Father and his priests are all imperfect
as you'd have them. What of that? Because there are no
perfect judges, is there no such thing as justice? Priests are
men, and since our father Adam fell imperfection has been
part of every man's essential nature. But it is accidental to
the Church which in its essence is, was and always will be
perfect.

RIZZIO: Brava! Multa brava!

KNOX (*smiles quite kindly*): Well now my lords, it seems we are
to have a little disputation here.

NAU: —No, no—

RIZZIO: —Yes—Avanti—Trounce him!

KNOX: What—Will you back your little fighting hen against
John Knox?

MARY: I am willing Master Knox.

KNOX (*kindly*): Good.

He turns away, looks over audience, manner musing, gentle, academic.

What is the essence of your Church, Your Grace?

MARY: Its essence?

KNOX: Aye. It is not, the Mass?

MARY: It is.

KNOX: What is this Mass?

MARY: It is the sacrament whereat the priest offers to God the sacrifice of Jesus Christ.

KNOX (*quickly, as not having heard*): Who offers it?

MARY: . . . It is a sacrament.

KNOX: Who offers it?

MARY: The priest.

KNOX: The priest . . .

His voice is not quite steady on the word. Then as before:

Without the sacrifice of Jesus Christ, could any soul hope for redemption?

MARY: No.

KNOX: Can God refuse that sacrifice, when it is offered?

MARY: He will not.

KNOX: Can he—?—(*Warning.*) Remembering that the Son who is sacrificed, the Father who is offered it are both—(*breathing hard now*)—one God?

MARY: . . . I see where you would lead me.

KNOX: Daren't you follow?

MARY: You are insolent!

KNOX: A very royal argument.

MARY: No. God cannot refuse it.

KNOX: Then God is at the mercy of the priest.

Murmur of satisfaction from the LORDS, *but* KNOX *ascends now to a level of frightening passion, though his voice is at first low.*

And my soul is at the mercy of the priest. For we can only traffic at the priest's permission. Christ's sacrifice is a cold spring, put here for my soul to drink at freely—which else must perish in this *desert* of a world! But now the Church has led this spring into a tank, and on this tank the priest has put a tap—the Mass—by which he turns Christ's mercy on and off and sells it by the dram!

MARY: Hold there—!

KNOX: Aye Madam, hold fast will I—for he will sell it into hands still red with the murder of a husband—

She leaps up from her chair.

—Hands still hot from groping, slake the thirst of carnal fever with it, ladle it down mouths still wet from filthy exercise, sell it will he—

MARY: Come down from there! By God come down or answer for your disobedience with your *head*!

KNOX: 'By God' *she says*, blaspheming in his very house!

MARY: This is no house of God! This is a market—where a scurrilous low peasant brings his dirty produce—!—(*Whirls on the* LORDS.) And buys treason from disloyal Lords!

NAU: Madam—!

KNOX (*tolerantly*): She is young. (*He descends.*)

MARY: Quit us!

KNOX: And passionate.

MARY: Go!

As he crosses, the LORDS *following:*

Ourselves we will to our own chapel—to hear Mass!

KNOX: Madam, I am sorry for you; make a marriage.

KNOX *and* LORDS *go, she crying after them:*

MARY: Save your sorrow for yourself John Knox! For I may make a marriage that will give this country cause for sorrow.

ALL *go. Light change. Fanfare modulates to Organ chord.*

BISHOP *and* CLERIC *enter, cross to pulpit, plain-chanting:*

BISHOP: God save the Queen.

CLERIC: And all the Royal Family.

BISHOP: God save the Duke and Duchess.

CLERIC: And both their charming children.

BISHOP: God save all Barons, Earls, Viscounts and Baronets.

CLERIC: And the ladies they have married.

BISHOP: God bless the Squire.

CLERIC: And the Squire's wife.

BISHOP: And the Squire's Bailiff.

CLERIC: And the Constable.

BISHOP: And the Overseer of the Highway.

CLERIC: And the Overseer of the Poor.

During this, they have replaced the Catholic cross and drape, been worried by the effect, replaced them with a more discreet cross and drape and congratulated one another. BISHOP *mounts into pulpit where now he concludes.*

BISHOP: God Bless all persons in positions of authority.

He smiles at his congregation and begins his address.

Steering our course between the Scylla of Rome and the Carybdis of Geneva, we in the Church of England cultivate the quality of moderation. Not one of the heroic virtues. No, compared with courage, and conviction, moderation is a modest matter. Sometimes—as I am aware—a laughing matter. Sobeit. The block and the bonfire are not laughing matters, and I would rather be the object of your ridicule than of your fear, will gladly spend Eternity in some quite humble mansion of my Father's House if I may get there without blood or fire . . . And that, at this point in our history is not so easy as you might suppose. No I am not ashamed to lift my voice and pray:

(Plain chant.) God Save the Queen.

DUDLEY, CECIL, CLERKS *enter. Plain chanting a descant.*

ALL: A-a-a-a-a-aaamen-en.

A blown up contemporary print of St James, labelled, flies in over table. DUDLEY *frontstage is adjusting a new robe and chain with fierce satisfaction.* CECIL *smiles.*

CECIL: Well sir Councillor, I said I should make your fortune.

DUDLEY: And that I should prove ungrateful. There you were wrong.

CECIL: We shall see. A word in your ear. Do not seem too ready in the business I have broached to you.

DUDLEY: No.

A VOICE (*off*): Ho there—the Queen!

CECIL: Let me persuade you.

DUDLEY: So.

> ELIZABETH *enters with* WALSINGHAM. *She affects surprise at seeing* DUDLEY.

ELIZABETH: How, Master Cecil, what does *this* fellow here?

> ALL *laugh at the Queen's little joke.*

DUDLEY (*kneels*): He kneels, serves, loves.

ELIZABETH: Well. Come then gentlemen.

> *They sit.* WALSINGHAM *busy with papers.*

WALSINGHAM: The New Dean for Durham. It is between Doctor Glover and Doctor Boze.

ELIZABETH: Which?

WALSINGHAM: Glover is three parts Catholic.

ELIZABETH: Walsingham for Doctor Boze.

CECIL: I also Madam. There are too many Catholics in the North already. Too close to the Border.

> WALSINGHAM *scribbles as:*

ELIZABETH: To the Lord Bishop at Durham. Reverend Father in God. We have heeded your request to name a person. Long thought and anxious prayer alike conclude in Doctor Boze. She that hath you ever in her mind and care, your loving Sovereign, Elizabeth etcetera.

> *As* CLERK *crosses with letter to* BISHOP *in pulpit she says to* DUDLEY.

You see how we dispatch here, Councillor.

> BISHOP *glances at paper.*

BISHOP: To the Queen's Majesty at St James. May it please Your Grace, this Doctor Boze inclines towards Geneva and the people hereabouts alas bend hard the other way. We fear he will prove contumaceous. May it please Your Grace to think upon the Reverend Doctor Culpepper.

> CLERIC *looks modest.*

This gentleman is moderate, learned, lowly, and discreet. He loves not dispute. Besides he is known to us.

Hands letter to CLERK *who takes it back to table,* CLERIC *and* BISHOP *looking anxiously after him,* BISHOP *murmuring:*

Eternally Your Grace's grateful servant Hugh, Dunelmiensis.

ELIZABETH: Reverenced Father. The multiplying merits of your nephew are known to us. Notwithstanding, further thought and yet extended prayer confirm our former choice. But we would not be peremptory.

BISHOP: It's Boze.

He sits, light down on pulpit.

WALSINGHAM: Good.

ELIZABETH: Glover is the better man.

CECIL: But Boze the better watchdog. And Your Grace has need of watchdogs on the Scottish Border, now.

ELIZABETH (*alert*): Why? What news from Scotland?

CECIL: It comes from Madrid, Your Grace. It is quite certain that the King of Spain will marry his son to Mary Stuart.

ELIZABETH: . . . Well then, it is certain.

CECIL: Your Grace, it must not be.

ELIZABETH: What then? (*He does not answer.*)

WALSINGHAM: It cannot be Your Grace; war rather.

CECIL: War with Spain . . .?

ELIZABETH: What then? Speak!

CECIL (*hesitates then*): Spain would not marry Scotland, if he could marry here.

ELIZABETH: Cecil, I have told you not to speak of this again.

CECIL: I spoke at Your command Your Grace.

ELIZABETH: Oh Cecil, you are too clever to be honest . . .

She rises, uneasy. CECIL *presses his advantage.*

CECIL: If a Spanish army comes at us from Scotland it comes through the Catholic North. On a Catholic Crusade, with a Catholic Queen at its head. And the North won't fight . . .

ELIZABETH: And would the South accept a Catholic King? Walsingham, would you?

All look at WALSINGHAM, *and* CECIL *quickly:*

CECIL: No King; a Consort.

WALSINGHAM: He would not be offered the Crown Matrimonial?

CECIL: No.

WALSINGHAM: And a Protestant marriage?

CECIL: Of course.

WALSINGHAM: It is a way, Your Grace. If he will take those terms.

ELIZABETH: He will not.

CECIL: Then give him war Your Grace, and then give even me a sword—but only then. And he would come by sea, we might resist. But if he comes by land what army can we send against those Spanish Infantry? We are Sunday bowmen; and they are men of iron; and they have proved themselves of such a sort that where they set their foot no grass grows, thereafter. War with Spain is England lost.

It makes a silence.

ELIZABETH: And the Prince of Spain is a dribbling dwarf! A diminutive monster who foams at the mouth!

CECIL: I cannot answer for his person, Majesty; I will answer for my policy.

DUDLEY *shifts.*

ELIZABETH: Aye, what do you think, Councillor Robin?

DUDLEY: Too much to speak, Your Grace.

ELIZABETH: Then quit my Council.

DUDLEY: Robin thinks, war rather, death rather, let England go. Your Grace's Councillor thinks no, let love go; Her Grace must keep England.

ELIZABETH *shifts, looks away; harshly:*

ELIZABETH: Love? Who spoke of love? . . . (*Holds out hand to* CECIL.) For Madrid. (*Glances at the paper which* CECIL *hands her.*) Who wrote this?

CECIL: I Your Grace.

ELIZABETH: We did not think you had such wooing terms.

CECIL: I was young once, Your Grace.

ELIZABETH: Logic compels us to believe you. For Madrid—

> MESSENGER *exits with letter.* DUDLEY'S *head sunk in apparent gloom.*

Cecil, what can I do for this gentleman?

CECIL: There was an Earl of Leicester once in England.

ELIZABETH: Earl—? You are very sudden friends.

CECIL: I hope it truly, Madam.

DUDLEY: Your Grace, I am not worthy.

ELIZABETH: Then be so, Lord Earl. (*Raises her voice.*) We will receive the King of Spain's reply at Hampton.

> CECIL *and* DUDLEY *rise and bow. St James flies out as Hampton Court flies in.* CECIL *and* DUDLEY *meanwhile meet frontstage, while* ELIZABETH *and* WALSINGHAM *'freeze'.*

CECIL: Well, sir, I had not thought you were so politic.

DUDLEY: Neither had I. I do not relish this.

CECIL: We dig for gold because we relish gold sir. Not because we relish digging. Do you want to break off?

DUDLEY: No.

CECIL: Come then. (*Leaving.*)

DUDLEY: What is my part this time?

CECIL: Perfect silence. Come.

> *They approach the table, bow together and together:*

CECIL:
DUDLEY: } Your Grace. (*And sit.*)

ELIZABETH: You arrive together, gentlemen.

CECIL: We met on the road, Your Grace. Is the Spanish Ambassador come?

ELIZABETH (*to* CLERK): Admit him.

> *Enter* DE QUADRA. *Crosses swiftly, kisses her hand with affectionate respect.*

ELIZABETH: De Quadra. How does your master?

DE QUADRA: Your Grace. His Catholic Majesty is all transported. He thinks Madrid a little town in Paradise. And only fears to have curtailed his future lot by tasting Heaven here.

ELIZABETH: We thank His Majesty. And, His Majesty's fair son?

DE QUADRA: His son! Your Grace, a heart of thistledown. He floats.

ELIZABETH: Then we shall float together; for we are even as you say he is.

DE QUADRA: *Madam* . . .

CECIL: What dowry does His Majesty propose?

DE QUADRA: Ah Cecil my good friend, the King would dower such a match with the whole world—

CECIL: —But failing that.

    DE QUADRA *whips out a roll of paper and places it deftly into* CECIL'S *hands, gliding on to* ELIZABETH *in the same movement.*

DE QUADRA: This (*a locket*) is a likeness of the Prince.

ELIZABETH: His Highness is well favoured, if this speaks true.

DE QUADRA: Would it might Your Grace, but alas it is not the handwork of a god.

ELIZABETH: De Quadra, such a face presages a strong mind.

DE QUADRA: Even so.

ELIZABETH: Deal honestly De Quadra.

DE QUADRA: Your Grace, His Highness it is true is—highly-strung—But there what would you—?—The spirit of a giant in a little human frame.

ELIZABETH: How little?

DE QUADRA: His Highness is compact Your Grace. I would not say *little* . . .

ELIZABETH: Would you say tall?

DE QUADRA: Tall . . . Alas Your Grace, how tall is tall?

ELIZABETH: This gentleman is tall.

    DUDLEY *rises.* CECIL *looks up from the scroll.*

CECIL: This is well.

DE QUADRA: I think so too, sir.

CECIL: Yet not so well that it could not be better. What is this of Spanish galleys in our Channel ports?

WALSINGHAM: What? That sounds more like war than wedding!

DE QUADRA: Ah, Master Walsingham, how do you do? (*To*

ELIZABETH.) The galleys are for use against His Majesty's rebellious subjects in the Netherlands.

WALSINGHAM: Our best trade is with the Netherlands, Your Grace.

DE QUADRA: It will be better, when the Netherlands are pacified.

WALSINGHAM: The Netherlanders are good friends to England, and to God.

DE QUADRA: With deference Master Walsingham, they may be your friends, God selects his own. And as for England—are rebel subjects anywhere good friends to any sovereign?

ELIZABETH: Spanish galleys in our ports might make me rebel subjects here, Your Excellency.

DE QUADRA: Well well. The galleys are a lesser matter.

ELIZABETH: You have a greater?

DE QUADRA: The form of marriage.

CECIL: English.

DE QUADRA: With a Catholic marriage first.
    It is half a question, half an assertion.

CECIL: After.

DE QUADRA: Then immediately after.

WALSINGHAM: Why immediately?

DE QUADRA (*shrug*): The same day.

WALSINGHAM: Why the same day?

DE QUADRA (*testy*): Before the *night* good Master Walsingham
    . . . In Catholic eyes your English form of marriage would be—
    (*Spreads his hands, delicately*)—a form.

WALSINGHAM: As would the Catholic form in English eyes.

DE QUADRA: *Some* English eyes.
    He says it significantly and looks at CECIL.

CECIL: Immediately after.

DE QUADRA: Excellent. The—er—form of the form is important too. Your Grace must know—for I alas am told to tell Your Grace—my master will not have his son's soul jeopardized by any form which makes a mock of God.

ELIZABETH: Then tell your master that we think ourselves as careful of our soul as any king in christendom and would permit no form which mocked at God!

DE QUADRA: Your English Church is, er, flexible Your Grace. Here it is one thing there another. Here a priest who is almost a Catholic there a priest who is no-one knows what. There have lately been some church appointments, as that of Doctor Boze at Durham, which have much dismayed my master.

ELIZABETH: Zounds sir, will you make our church appointments now?

DE QUADRA: Oh dear. Of course these vexious questions would not be, if His Highness were to wed some Catholic Queen.

He lets it hang. CECIL *and* DUDLEY *look at* ELIZABETH. *She sighs, raises voice and:*

ELIZABETH: To the Lord Bishop at Durham!

Lights up on pulpit. BISHOP *attentive.*

Reverend Father in God. We have reconsidered your wise words concerning Doctor Boze. The man is disputatious. If therefore it is not too late, appoint instead the Reverend Doctor Glover—

BISHOP: Glover—!—Your Grace the man's a rampant Papist!

ELIZABETH: —You see from this that weighed against her care for you and for the spiritual welfare of her realm, no sacrifice of vain consistency is too much for your loving Sovereign, Elizabeth, etcetera.

BISHOP: The woman's mad!

Lights out on pulpit as he sits.

DE QUADRA: Excellent. And who can say but that the tender influence of love will heal up these unhappy differences, his golden dart transfixing two young hearts make one of two great kingdoms. The galleys are a matter for negotiation, naturally.

CECIL: Naturally.

DE QUADRA: May I enjoy your company tonight?

CECIL: Tonight I am engaged, Your Excellency.

DE QUADRA: Tomorrow then?

CECIL: Tomorrow I shall be in Canterbury.

DE QUADRA: Well let us not delay too long. Youth will be served. Your Grace I go now to write that which will transport my master; would I had words worthy of my theme. (*He makes a graceful bow and to* CECIL, *backing:*) Next week perhaps?

CECIL: Your Excellency's servant.

DE QUADRA: Madam, you have made me happy. (*Another bow.*)

ELIZABETH: Then we are quits.

DE QUADRA: Madam. (*Another bow; he is almost gone.*)

ELIZABETH: Your Excellency. (*He stops.*) We had thought your Prince had lost his heart to the Queen of Scots.

DE QUADRA: The—? Your Grace, the Queen of Scots. Who remembers the pale moon, when the great sun rises?

    A final bow, and he is gone.

ELIZABETH: Well, Cecil, will it do?

CECIL: I do not know, Your Grace.

WALSINGHAM: Nor I, Your Grace. I think they mean to make us clients.

ELIZABETH: I think it will not do. And thank God for it.

CECIL: Madam, it must seem to do; until the Queen of Scots has married elsewhere.

ELIZABETH: Then let her marry soon.

CECIL: I think she will.

ELIZABETH: Perhaps we can arrange a marriage for her.

CECIL: That would be best Your Grace. I have intelligence from Scotland coming to Nonsuch.

ELIZABETH: Mp. To Nonsuch then.

    Hampton out. Nonsuch in. DUDLEY *and* CECIL *front stage.* ELIZABETH *and* WALSINGHAM *'freeze'.*

CECIL: Well, my lord, the dice are falling in our favour. Are you ready for your final throw?

DUDLEY: Cecil, why are you doing this?

CECIL: Because it is good policy for England.

DUDLEY: And what is it for Cecil?

CECIL: Good policy too. You have her heart and always will.

DUDLEY grips him hard by the arm and growls desperately.

DUDLEY: Then why may I not marry *here*?

CECIL: That, over my grave; the other I will help you to. Will you have it?

DUDLEY (*drops his hand*): Yes.

CECIL: To it then. You that way, I this.

They approach the table from different directions and meet there.

DUDLEY (*sitting*): Well met Master Cecil.

CECIL: My lord. (*Sitting.*)

ELIZABETH: How is de Quadra?

CECIL: He languishes a little, but we keep him in good heart. We feed him promises.

ELIZABETH: 'We'?

CECIL: My lord had dinner with de Quadra and myself the other day.

ELIZABETH: You are grown quite intimate.

CECIL (*with a little laugh and half bow to* DUDLEY): Oh, I—would not say 'intimate'.

ELIZABETH: You sound like de Quadra. Admit the messenger from Scotland.

Enter DAVISON. *He kneels. She regards him approvingly, motions him to rise.*

So sir, the Spanish embassy to Scotland is gone home.

DAVISON: Yes Your Grace.

ELIZABETH: And how likes that the Queen of Scots?

DAVISON: She is enraged Your Grace.

ELIZABETH (*a grunt of satisfaction*): Ha. And does her rage become her?

DAVISON: Yes Your Grace. All moods become her.

He says it defiantly. She stares and:

ELIZABETH: God's death, send no more *young* ambassadors to Scotland, Cecil.

She gets up, goes and examines DAVISON *as an object of deep, half-amused interest.*

ELIZABETH: Describe her then.

DAVISON: Your Grace, I cannot.

ELIZABETH: Cannot? Is she tall?

DAVISON: As Your Grace.

ELIZABETH: Thin?

DAVISON: As Your Grace.

ELIZABETH: We are twins?

DAVISON: No Your Grace.

ELIZABETH: What colour is her hair?

DAVISON: Your Grace her hair is shadow coloured.

ELIZABETH: God's death, he's written poetry. Her eyes?

DAVISON: Her eyes change colour with her moods Your Grace.

ELIZABETH: You seem much taken with her moods. Has she many?

DAVISON: Yes Your Grace.

ELIZABETH: Aye, sometimes she is right childish, is she not?

DAVISON: Yes Your Grace. And sometimes—(*Breaks off.*)

ELIZABETH: Well?

DAVISON: Right royal; Your Grace.

ELIZABETH: Hoo! And sometimes, as we hear, she is sportive, hey? Gallante, hey? Wanton?

DAVISON: Yes Your Grace. And cruel and wilful and unfair. But then there come such sudden sinkings, such declension into soft submission, as sets a man on a high horse.

His voice vibrates with an emotion too serious to laugh away. She leaves him, on a shaky laugh.

ELIZABETH: God's death it ought not to be hard to find a suitor for the lady, Cecil.

She turns to find CECIL *and* DUDLEY *making furious faces at* DAVISON. CECIL *with fists raised above his head. He converts the motion hastily into a stroking of his hair as she turns, but she:*

ELIZABETH: What? What's this?

Looks at DAVISON.

What? (*Snort of mirth.*) You think we are jealous of this moon calf?

She seats herself. More formally:

What is this mountebank, Rizzio?

DAVISON: Her playfellow, Your Grace.

ELIZABETH: No more?

DAVISON: Her Councillor, Your Grace.

ELIZABETH: No more?

DAVISON: I do not know, Your Grace. But I do not think he is the man that she would love.

ELIZABETH: Why not? Come, we are not angry with you. (*She smiles.*) Why is Signor Rizzio not the man that she would love? Is he ugly?

DAVISON: It is not that Your Grace. (*He looks at her and ventures a half-smile in response to hers.*) He is small.

ELIZABETH: Ah . . . like you.

She goes to him and rubs his hair.

The Queen of Scots likes tall men does she?

MESSENGER: Yes Your Grace.

ELIZABETH: Poor boy. (*Then briskly, cheerfully:*) Well then Master Cecil it seems that we are looking for a tall—

Breaks off and freezes. The life drains from her motionless body. She looks at CECIL, *at* DUDLEY, *back to* CECIL. *He bows his head. She comprehends it all. She looks away. White-faced she breathes out:*

O-o-o-oh . . .

She looks quickly at DUDLEY *with a last flash of hope. But now he too bows his head and again:*

O-o-o-oh . . .

Her empty eyes wander to DAVISON.

You sir, get you gone; you are love-sick.

He goes.

Oh, Cecil.

CECIL: Your Grace—

ELIZABETH: I *see* it, Cecil, I *see* it's very good. Protestant, English, loyal, a nobleman to boot—Earl of Leicester. And, tall . . . It should do well . . . Eh . . .? Robin?

DUDLEY: Your Grace I am green in Council—these gentlemen are better able—

ELIZABETH: —*Faugh*—!

She gestures.

Go.

DUDLEY *going.*

Go both.

CECIL *follows. They escape like schoolboys. She gently contemplates.*

Oh Robin . . .

WALSINGHAM *discreetly gathering papers, going.*

You are going, sir?

WALSINGHAM: I thought Your Grace might wish to stay this business until . . . (*His voice tails.*)

ELIZABETH: Do you presume to know what we might wish?

He sits, very quietly.

What business?

WALSINGHAM: A conspiracy against Your Grace's life, of Catholic gentlemen, in the County of Durham.

ELIZABETH: Against my life?

WALSINGHAM: Yes Your Grace.

ELIZABETH: Well. Tell Cecil.

WALSINGHAM: Your Grace. (*Going.*)

ELIZABETH: In the county of Durham?

WALSINGHAM: Yes Your Grace.

She nods. He goes. She looks at DUDLEY's empty chair.

ELIZABETH: Oh . . . Councillor . . .

She raises her head and softly begins. Softly lights come up on pulpit and the gravely listening BISHOP there.

To the Lord Bishop at Durham. Good Father we trouble you much. But both the gentlemen that we have named are too extreme, for this time, and that place. Therefore, let it be your kinsman's. For you tell us that he is a man of balance. And we are like a sleepwalker who wakes to find herself on a high roof, in darkness . . . and without a hand to hold her. Forgive, Elizabeth, etcetera . . .

She is going out on the last words, her hand just momentarily placed on DUDLEY'S *chair before passing on as* BISHOP *hurries down from pulpit, subdued but urgent:*

BISHOP: May it please Your Grace, my nephew is gone from here and is presently in Bristol where—

ELIZABETH (*ringingly*): Lord Bishop!

She whirls.

Do as we command or by God we will unfrock you!

She takes a great gasp of air and almost shouts:

Elizabeth! Queen!

Fanfare; she exits. Hampton flies out. Fanfare. Light change; MARY *enters. She is on* CECIL'S *arm.* NAU, LADIES, *and* RIZZIO *follow. She seats herself.*

MARY: Cecil you are very welcome. We hear you are the wisest Councillor in Christendom. We think our cousin kind to part with you. The moreso as we know her pleasant purpose.

CECIL: Your Grace, her purpose is most pleasant, yes.

MARY: Aye, for you are sent we hear to crack a joke with us. But we must warn you sir the edge is off it, for it is foretold.

CECIL: A joke Your Grace?

MARY: Oh. Davie, we are misinformed. Forgive me sir. There was a waggish fellow here the other day who said your purpose was to offer me the hand of Robert Dudley.

CECIL: Madam, that is my purpose.

MARY: How straight he keeps his face. Excellent, sir. If you were not a Councillor you could be a comedian.

CECIL: Indeed Your Grace I so lack comedy I cannot understand how you can find the offer comic.

MARY: Sir, do not persist. Your offer is an insult—

CECIL: Your Grace?

MARY: Cecil, was Robert Dudley unfit for Elizabeth? And yet is fit for me?

CECIL: Nay now I am quite confounded. Unfit for my mistress?

She never thought of him Your Grace. He has her high regard indeed but, no no, not her heart.

MARY: No, that she has given to the Prince of Spain.

CECIL: That is correct Your Grace.

MARY: We wish him joy of such a heart. We wish her joy of such a husband. And for her comfort tell your mistress that we have given our heart to an Englishman.

CECIL: . . . May I know his name?

MARY: His name is Darnley.

CECIL: Now it is Your Grace who jests I hope, for if this is not jest it is high treason.

MARY: Sir, I am a sovereign and can commit no treason unless against myself.

CECIL: You will find that you have done that Madam, if you wed Lord Darnley. I have seen the man, Your Grace has not —he is a ladyfaced horseman, empty and idle.

MARY: Oh—It is on our account that you oppose it? We thank you for your care.

CECIL: My opposition matters nothing Madam but my mistress has forbidden it; for reasons you know well.

MARY: I do not study Elizabeth's reasons. But can guess them. Lord Darnley is a Catholic.

CECIL: Yes Madam.

MARY: And bears the Tudor blood.

CECIL: Yes Madam.

MARY: Aye—and better Tudor blood than hers because it is legitimate.

CECIL: Madam, you forget yourself.

MARY: I forget nothing. England remembers more than you suppose, and Europe knows that any child of mine by Darnley would be heir to the English throne. These are Elizabeth's reasons. And mine.

CECIL: Well Madam I am sorry for it. And I council you to put it from your mind. Lord Darnley is forbidden to quit England and will not come if you call him.

MARY: Call him.

NAU: Lord Darnley.

> DARNLEY *enters.* CECIL *aghast. Then softly:*

CECIL: You fool . . .

MARY: Quit Scotland, sir, you are an uncouth messenger.

> CECIL *bows curtly, going, stopped by:*

And tell your mistress that I have one reason more than she. (*Takes* DARNLEY'*s hand.*) I love this bonny gentleman.

CECIL: I think you are deceived Your Grace. I think that you are angry with my mistress. That bonny gentleman is light. And I think that when you are undeceived you will find his passing heavy.

MARY: God's death, sir, have you finished?

CECIL: That is for Your Grace to say.

MARY: You have finished.

> CECIL *goes, escorted by* NAU *and* RIZZIO.

MARY: Well, if that was Cecil, Elizabeth is welcome to him. Good lord I think she must have run him up from odds and ends left over from a funeral.

DARNLEY: I thought he spoke well.

MARY: He is a politician, Harry, speaking well's his trade. You were not moved by what he said?

DARNLEY: Weren't you?

MARY: I have forgotten what he said.

DARNLEY: He called me fool and said I was not fit for you.

MARY: The more fool he.

DARNLEY: Nay, all the world accounts him wise—and me unfit for you.

MARY: My love, I have not found you so—

DARNLEY: You have not wished to find me so.

MARY: You are too thoughtful sir.

DARNLEY: I never was accounted that.

MARY: Then what has made you so? Is it my rank?

DARNLEY: My breeding fits me for your rank. Yourself has made me thoughtful.

MARY: Oh. If thought is all I have roused in you, I have wasted many pains.

DARNLEY: Nay, you have roused my love.

MARY: Be careless then, not thoughtful. You know that I love you.

DARNLEY: I know you would.

MARY: Harry, I have told you, and I swear before the Saints: I'll have a husband I can love, or else I will have none at all.

DARNLEY: Would you have loved the Prince of Spain?

MARY: Nay do not shame me, love. That was to have been a stroke of State. Yet Harry, even him I would have tried to love.

DARNLEY: And now you are trying to love me.

MARY: My lord, we were so born that we must choose fit marriage mates politically. It is God's generosity that we have found fit mates we naturally love. We are not to scrutinize his generosity, we are to love. If we attend to love my lord both dignity and reputation will come begging at our door.

Uplifted he goes to her. They kiss.

Oh come my love—and let's be married!

Bells, cheering and cheerful organ on speaker. She takes him by the hand and leads him towards the upper level. RIZZIO, NAU, LADIES *enter one side,* LORDS *the other.* MARY *and* DARNLEY *kneel, facing. Rise and kiss. Court applauding, crescendo on speaker. But the* LORDS *deliberately straddle their legs and fold their arms, glowering.*

MARY: My lords. Will you not rejoice?

MORTON: We have no cause here to rejoice.

MARY: Are even weddings not rejoiced at then, in Scotland?

MORTON: Your Grace is wedded to a Catholic boy.

DARNLEY: Call me 'boy' and you shall have cause for regret Lord Morton.

MORTON laughs.

What sir, do you laugh?

MORTON: Yes, I laugh.

DARNLEY: I never endured insult when I was a private man Lord
    Morton; do you think I will endure it now?
MORTON: Why, what are you now?
DARNLEY: By God sir, am I not your Lord?
MORTON: You are this lady's laddie; and no more.
DARNLEY: —Zounds—!
    He steps forward; MARY *stops him.*
MARY: —Harry—!—No—!
DARNLEY: What, am I to rule Scotland and must eat such stuff
    as this?
    A little silence, then MARY, *awkwardly:*
MARY: You are to rule me, my lord, not Scotland.
    DARNLEY *glares at her. Bows stiffly. Turns his back and goes.*
    She half starts after him.
Harry—!
    MORTON *laughs again. She whirls.*
Lord Morton. My Consort and myself mean you no harm.
And we will give ourselves one season in which to show we
mean no harm. Thereafter, we expect to see you smile . . .
Harry!
    She hurries after DARNLEY, *court following pell-mell.*
MORTON: Ten English pounds to ten Scots pennies, they're at
    one another's throats within six months.
RUTHVEN: No bet.
    LORDS *go, laughing. Light change.* ELIZABETH *enters at speed,*
    CECIL *after. She checks. He, diffident and soothing.*
CECIL (*placating*): Your Grace of course may marry whom you
    will.
ELIZABETH: Oh—!—You are full of news this morning, sir.
CECIL: Within what's reasonable—And this petition, which
    your loving Commons most respectfully present—
ELIZABETH: —Is no petition, but an admonition! I am
    admonished, by the Commons, to marry—now. Not when I
    would, nay nor to whom I would, but to one of these that
    they have named, and get a child by him—and now!

CECIL: The Princes they have named they have enquired into most—

ELIZABETH: Enquired, sir—? Are they kennelmen and I their breeding bitch?

CECIL: You are their mistress Madam and this country's Queen.

ELIZABETH: In this I am no more than any other woman, Cecil. And I tell you that I have nor mind, nor heart, to marry now.

CECIL: Your Grace it would be very prudent, now. The Queen of Scots expects a child.

ELIZABETH (*alert*): How do you know?

CECIL: I have it from Lord Morton, Madam.

ELIZABETH: He has written?

CECIL: He is here, Your Grace.

ELIZABETH: Fetch him.

He gestures quietly into wings. MORTON *enters.*

Is this true?

MORTON: Yes, Your Grace.

ELIZABETH: She has not announced it.

MORTON: No doubt she expects to make some use of the announcement.

CECIL: She'd be a fool if she did not expect to make some use of it—It is a useful thing.

ELIZABETH: If it is so.

MORTON: I have it from a friend who is a friend of a close lady-friend of Signor Rizzio.

ELIZABETH *picks up the petition, thoughtful.*

ELIZABETH: Is he still close friends with your Queen?

MORTON: He's been no more than that since she was married. But he is still that. It's true enough Your Grace.

ELIZABETH: I thought that Mary and her husband were no longer bedfellows.

MORTON: They're not, not since he took to whores. But they were busy bedfellows at first.

CECIL *looks at* ELIZABETH *expecting her to follow the main issue. But she is looking down and now looking up:*

ELIZABETH: It's true is it, that he has taken up with whores?

MORTON: Oh aye, and common brothel whores at that.

ELIZABETH: Why?

MORTON: He's a King in a brothel. In Council he's a clown. She boxed his ears and sent him packing from the Council in the end.

ELIZABETH: She boxed his ears?

MORTON: She all but pitched him off his seat.

ELIZABETH (*shrugs*): No wonder then he took to whores.

MORTON: Her wits go out the window when she's in a rage. And she was in a hellish rage. He showed so cocky and so daft you see, so brainless—overbearing, and so greedy for his own. And she, then, was in love with him.

ELIZABETH: She never was in love with him.

MORTON: Oh yes she was Your Grace.

ELIZABETH: She was infatuated.

MORTON: Your Grace may call it what you like. I saw it. She hung upon him like a pedler's bag. And sometimes when they danced, she had a look upon her face, that showed as much of her as if she had been naked . . . (*He is lost for a moment.*) No woman ever looked at me like that . . .

> CECIL *coughs*. MORTON *comes to*.

MORTON: She's three months gone.

CECIL: And she is nightly on her knees Your Grace and praying for a son. And praying for her son to be a wise and potent Prince. Of Scotland and of England too. As he is like to be, and soon Your Grace, unless Your Gr—

ELIZABETH: Enough, enough, I am not blind.

> *She looks at the petition.*

This is not ill-considered neither. But here they name three Catholic Princes and three Protestant. (*Puts down the petition.*) And if I go a courting any one of these, I lose the love of one half of my people.

CECIL: Your Grace may find that one half of your Court is paying court in Edinburgh presently!

She looks at him.

ELIZABETH: Do you pay court in Edinburgh?

CECIL: No Madam, I do not.

ELIZABETH: The time may come. Meanwhile tell the Commons that we will not marry, yet, but that we thank them for their care. And will remit some portion of the taxes due to us this coming year. I go a-courting with my people, Cecil.

She is going. He, irritated and anxious:

CECIL: And the son that she is praying for?

ELIZABETH: Why, on your knees good William and pray for it to be a girl. Three Queens on the run should finish any country.

She goes, leaving CECIL *perplexed.*

MORTON: That lassie has a long head on her shoulders.

CECIL (*preoccupied*): Yes . . . The problem is to keep it there.

MORTON: Well that may be a problem for us all, quite soon.

CECIL: It will. (*He looks at* MORTON, *who says nothing.*) So what do you intend to do Lord Morton?

MORTON (*wolfish grin*): Me, Master Cecil? D'you really want to know?

CECIL: Perhaps not. Good-day to you Lord Morton. (*Going.*)

MORTON: Good day to you.

    CECIL, *gone.*

You creepy wee creature.

He turns, joins Scots LORDS *who enter.* LADIES, RIZZIO, NAU *enter opposite. Then Fanfare.* MARY *enters, all bowing, mounts to upper level, addresses* LORDS, *smiling graciously.*

MARY: My lords, we have assembled you to hear a happy thing. You were right melancholy wedding guests but now I think you will rejoice. My lords, we are with child.

MORTON: And why should we rejoice at that?

MARY: Because you are loyal Scots.

MORTON: Aye we are Scots. And we should have a Scottish King.

MARY: If God grants me a son, you'll have a Scottish King.

MORTON: His mother for a start is French.

MARY: Sacre bleu . . .

She turns away impatiently but then turns back.

My father bore the blood of Bruce. And I was born at Lithgow Castle. When I was five years old I do confess I went away to France and got my breeding there—Forgive me, it was an error of my youth. If it's offensive that my manner is still Frenchified, sobeit and good-night, I can no more. It is not for myself I ask your loyalty. My child, on whose behalf I do demand your loyalty, will be both born and bred in Edinburgh —And fully Scots as you.

MORTON: And will he so?

MARY: By parentage it's true he'll be a little French on one side, a little English on the other—

MORTON: And will he so? By parentage?

MARY: I do not think I understand you, sir.

MORTON: I think you do. Where is Lord Darnley?

MARY: I do not know sir where he is.

MORTON: It's odd that he's not here.

MARY: It's very odd, I did desire him to be here.

MORTON: What means his being elsewhere then?

MARY: I cannot guess his meanings, but by Heaven I will come at yours.

MORTON: My meaning is the same as his. And you can come at it in any pub in Edinburgh. This child my lords will be a little French on one side, aye, but on the other—(*glares at* RIZZIO)—half Italian!

MARY raises a hand as though to strike him, controls herself, turns away.

RIZZIO: My lords—I swear by all the Saints—!—

MARY: What—? Will you protest it? Lord Morton leave us. You pollute the air.

MORTON and LORDS bow, go. She turns.

Well Claud, I have tried the patient way—

V.V.R.—3*

RIZZIO: —Maria.

He points warningly. She turns to find that BOTHWELL *has lingered and stands now looking at her. She is a bit startled.*

MARY: Lord Bothwell.

BOTHWELL (*bows gravely*): Your Grace.

MARY: What do you want?

BOTHWELL: A private audience.

MARY: Private? Why so?

BOTHWELL: Don't be frightened.

MARY: Frightened sir? What should I fear? Leave us gentlemen.

NAU (*anxious*): Your Grace it is not—

MARY: Nay leave us, Claud.

RIZZIO (*dubious*): Maria—

MARY: Va t'en.

   NAU, RIZZIO, LADIES, *go.* BOTHWELL *and* MARY *cross, slowly, eyeing one another.*

Well?

BOTHWELL: Puir wee lass.

MARY (*amused and startled*): What?

BOTHWELL: You're going to have a hard confinement. You're too thin for it, though.

MARY: Indeed?

BOTHWELL: I know what I'm talking about too. You just bide quiet awhile. Don't ride so much; and don't ride so wild. And mind what you're eatin'. And altogether be a bit more sensible; and treat yourself more kind.

MARY: Well thanks; I will.

BOTHWELL: Guid. When's it due?

MARY: The time of our confinement is a thing we will announce when we are minded to Lord Bothwell.

BOTHWELL: July.

MARY: Who told you that?

BOTHWELL: It wasn't very hard to guess—Your husband has been spending himself elsewhere since November, has he not?

MARY: If you will speak of him sir you will study your respect.

BOTHWELL: Let's speak of something else then. You'd have to study hard to speak of Darnley with respect.

MARY: I think this insolence is studied. Leave us.

BOTHWELL: Look, I have matter which you ought to hear.

MARY: I will not hear it.

He shrugs and is about to go.

Unless you can attain a minimum of manner too.

BOTHWELL: Sacre bleu! (*Mimics her.*) If my manner is offensive sobeit and good-night.

MARY: Oh Jesus are we there again?

BOTHWELL: I like your manner fine.

She looks at him.

It's very pretty.

MARY: Good heavens my Lord that is the second compliment within these same four years.

BOTHWELL: Now fancy you rememberin' the first.

MARY: Remember it—? How not? A compliment in Scotland is a memorable thing. It stands out like a lily on a heap of dung.

BOTHWELL: That's no' a bad description of yourself in Scotland.

They exchange a little mocking bow.

MARY: I'll hear your matter.

BOTHWELL: It's men and means you want I think?

MARY: It is.

BOTHWELL: You do not mean to meddle with the Kirk?

MARY: The Kirk, sir? Are you pious?

BOTHWELL: When the Kirk threw down the Catholic Church I got some fine broad meadow land; that used to belong to the Catholic Church. I'm awfu' pious about those meadows.

MARY: If I got men and means from you, I could not meddle with your meadows.

BOTHWELL: That's true enough. What terms are you offerin'?

MARY: No terms. I have taken out an option on the future Bothwell; and you have wit enough to see it.

BOTHWELL (*smiling approval*): You're no fool are you?

MARY: No sir; did you think I was?

BOTHWELL: You married Darnley.

MARY: . . . What is it in me Bothwell that provokes you and your fellow lords at every turn and all the time to strip me of my dignity? Is it merely that I am a woman?

BOTHWELL: A bonny woman.

MARY: So?

BOTHWELL: Worth strippin'.

MARY: Is that another compliment?

BOTHWELL: Yes.

MARY: Your vein of courtesy's exhausted. Go.

> BOTHWELL *going*.

It was a compliment sir for a courtesan.

BOTHWELL: Am I to go or stay?

MARY: You'll change your ways, sir if you stay.

BOTHWELL: I have no mind to change my ways. We're very much alike.

MARY: You will not tell me that's a compliment.

BOTHWELL: Oh I steal sheep and you steal revenues. Otherwise we're much alike.

MARY: By God there is another difference—

BOTHWELL: —There is—

MARY: —I am a sovereign. And you sir are a subject.

BOTHWELL: No. You are a woman. (*Approaches close.*) Why don't you send me packin' now?

MARY: Oh sir I am fascinated by your rough provincial masculinity.

BOTHWELL: I think you are, a bit.

MARY: Go!

> BOTHWELL *going again*.

You are unfit for our purpose.

BOTHWELL: Why what was that?

MARY: What sir, do you smell promotion?

BOTHWELL: Do I?

MARY: A high promotion Bothwell; you might come by further meadows.

BOTHWELL: What then?

MARY: We had thought to make you Lord Protector to our child.

BOTHWELL: Oh. (*He pulls at his beard, thoughtfully.*)

MARY: Ay. Now I think he'll change his ways.

BOTHWELL: You'd want a Catholic for that.

MARY: So change your church and be a Catholic. It would not cost you much.

BOTHWELL: It would not cost me anything, to be a Catholic, for I am not a Christian. I will not do it though. For if our ways are different and you would like our ways to match— you must change your ways! To mine!

MARY: By Heaven Lord Bothwell I have heard about your ways —Even in Scotland your name is morbid. You are a bloody villain sir, a tyrant and a sodomist, an enemy to innocence, a vampire and a demonist! It's only in your better moments Bothwell that you are a thief.

BOTHWELL: So *that's* what fascinates you.

MARY: Go!

He goes.

MARY: And go for ever—be banished to Dunbar—You will never see my face again!

BOTHWELL: You're wrong I think.

MARY: *Go!*

BOTHWELL: I was goin'—you keep stoppin' me.

He has gone. She glares after him. Unseen behind her NAU *and* RIZZIO *enter.*

MARY: Lout!

RIZZIO: Bothwell?

MARY: Yes. (*Turns to him with a little laugh.*) I do believe he thinks he is a lady's man!

RIZZIO: Astonishing.

MARY: No fooling sir; I am not in the mood.

Light begins to concentrate into a small conspiratorial area at the table surrounded by shadow. She sits, and says to NAU:

Did any other of the lords come forward, Claud?

NAU: No Your Grace.

MARY (*dips pen*): Well . . . (*She writes rapidly.*) I will try my way now.

He sits and watches her unhappily. RIZZIO *too draws near.*

NAU: You write, Your Grace?

MARY: Yes sir, I write.

RIZZIO (*peeping*): In Latin too.

NAU: To whom does Your Grace write?

RIZZIO: He'll have difficulty reading it, whoever he may be.

MARY (*writing*): So you will make it fair. And you (*looking up at* NAU) will carry it to Rome.

NAU (*sadly*): Oh Madam, Rome?

MARY: And when you have got means, in Rome, I will send to Milan, for mercenaries. Loyalty does not grow in Scotland, so I will import it.

DARNLEY *enters, uncertainly, hanging off in the shadows.*

NAU: My lord.

DARNLEY (*eagerly*): Good evening, Claud . . . Signor Rizzio.

RIZZIO: My lord.

They withdraw respectfully as he drifts towards MARY, *who after one glance round, one stare, has returned to her writing. He sits and watches her.*

DARNLEY: Good evening, Mary.

MARY: What do you want?

DARNLEY: Might I not simply have come home, like any other man?

MARY: You might. It seems improbable.

She has not looked up from her flying pen. A pause:

DARNLEY: Are you writing a letter?

MARY: Yes.

DARNLEY: Who to?

She thrusts it towards him at full stretch. He looks at it.

It's in Latin.

MARY: Yes.

DARNLEY: I can't read Latin.

MARY: No.

She pulls it back and goes on writing.

DARNLEY: You're cruel, Mary.

MARY: Oh Harry, go away.

DARNLEY: Mary, I'm sorry.

It is touching in its sincerity, pathetic in its infantile inadequacy. She shifts restlessly, and stops writing but doesn't look up, exhaustedly impatient:

MARY: Have you been drinking?

DARNLEY: I'm not drunk.

MARY: You're maudlin'.

DARNLEY: It isn't drink that's made me maudlin as you call it. Not this evening.

He waits. She struggles against it, but:

MARY: What is it then? (*She still hasn't looked up.*)

DARNLEY (*pathetically*): Mary . . .

MARY (*exasperated*): What?

DARNLEY: Look at me.

She blows out an angry sigh throws down pen and raises her glowering face. But seeing him, her expression alters. She rises, staring, backs away. RIZZIO *and* NAU *come forward alarmed.* DARNLEY *averts his face from them.*

NAU: Your Grace.

MARY: There are sores on his mouth . . . Harry, look at me— What are those sores on your mouth?

Her reaction has appalled him, he rises, stares wildly at RIZZIO *and* NAU *and then defiantly:*

DARNLEY: It's the frost!

MARY: By God I know that frost—Stand off—! (*He has approached.*)

DARNLEY: Mary—

MARY: Sir will you not stand off? You are unclean—!

He almost runs to Exit, turns, and in a voice shaking with feeling.

DARNLEY: . . . God save me from a loving woman.

He goes. She starts after him.

MARY: Harry . . . (*She checks.*) Oh Jesus—the child . . .!

RIZZIO goes to her, alert and calm.

RIZZIO: When was the child conceived, Maria?

MARY: Four—four and a half months.

RIZZIO: And have you seen the sores before?

MARY: No?

RIZZIO: The child is safe.

MARY: Oh Davie, do you really know?

RIZZIO: Indeed. In Padua this useful branch of knowledge was the most highly regarded of my many accomplishments. I was greatly in demand. But do you know I have never been so greatly in demand as I have since we came to this godly city of Edinburgh? I think it is the cold you know, it brings people together . . . Ah good, you laugh. And the child is safe.

MARY: Thank God for Davie.

RIZZIO: I do, frequently.

She smiles again, but then her smile fades.

MARY: And . . . him?

RIZZIO: Your husband. Hm. The English have a saying: You have made your bed and you must lie in it. Myself I have never seen the need for this; when there are other beds.

She drifts towards Exit. Turns, looks at him, then softly.

MARY: Davie, bring your lute.

She goes. RIZZIO, *delicately, rising:*

RIZZIO: Aha!

NAU: Signor Rizzio—Don't go to her!

RIZZIO: Oh come Claud, the Queen needs (*He makes a deliberately ambiguous gesture.*) . . . Comfort.

He goes after MARY. NAU *goes separately.* LORDS *enter. Tramp across to table.* MORTON *picks up letter.*

MORTON: Who here has lands from the old Church?

ALL: I.

MORTON: Well you're to lose them.

RUTHVEN: Ach, she hasnae the men.

MORTON: Oh she'll have taken thought for that. It'll be French-
men maybe, or maybe mercenaries, but no no she thought of
that before she did this. (*Puts it down.*) So what's to do?

RUTHVEN: Fight.

MORTON: It's gey expensive fightin'. An' you can always lose.

RUTHVEN: What then?

*From behind the curtain at head of the shallow pyramid of stairs,
the sound of the lute, playing* RIZZIO'S *tune. They turn and look.
Light begins to gather, ominous.*

MORTON: I'm getting to like that instrument. Verra seductive.
Aye—a bagpipe's gey stirrin' on the moors but it's no help in
a bedroom.

RUTHVEN: What are you talking about?

MORTON: Her husband you gowk.

LINDSEY: Why what can *he* do?

MORTON: Nothing while he's only that. But suppose he was the
King. And suppose he was bound to us. Bound hard. Our
man.

LINDSEY: He's no a man at all.

MORTON: Well call him a man for courtesy. D'you see it?

RUTHVEN: No.

MORTON: Well I do Ruthven. I see it clear. So either come
with me or take yourself off and be damned.

RUTHVEN: I'll come with you.

MORTON: Right, here he is.

DARNLEY *enters, as before but without the bottle.* MORTON
sotto, urgent:

Give him a bow, give him a bow.

They bow. DARNLEY *stops uncertainly.*

DARNLEY: My lords? . . .

MORTON. You look sick sir. Are you?

DARNLEY: Yes.

MORTON: And so are we sir of the same disease.

DARNLEY: What?

MORTON: Domination! Domination by a woman. That we are sick of, and so is Scotland.

DARNLEY: By God you are right, Morton; that is my sickness.

MORTON: We know it sir. We have watched you. And we think you are too patient. We think the husband of the Queen should be a King.

DARNLEY (*looks at them, breathing hard, pulling at his opened doublet, trying to sober up*): Well?

MORTON: And you would be the King, sir, you must play the leader.

DARNLEY: Leader?

MORTON: Aye. And if you'd be a husband, you must play the man!

The lute again; a low laugh from MARY.

Ha! They're vigorous enough, heh? They're diligent, heh?

DARNLEY: Wha'—?

MORTON: God's death my lord, they're going *to* it—now!

DARNLEY: Who—?

MORTON: The monkey—! And your wife!

DARNLEY: *Whaaa-aa*—!

He reels towards the steps, MORTON *grips him by the arm and wheels him round and back. Admiring chuckle.*

MORTON: Did I not say there was a kingly spirit in this man? But see Your Majesty, these things must be done majestically. I have here a wee paper. Which all of us will sign.

He puts it on the table. Curt nod to his colleagues.

Sign.

As they do:

DARNLEY: What is it?

MORTON: Our warrant.

DARNLEY: Warrant?

MORTON: Aye—or say a promise which we make each to each

other, aye and God Almighty too that what we purpose here
is a naething mair nor less than justice for yourself and David
Rizzio; nae mair for you nae less for him. The crown for the
King, death for the adulterer. Now you sign.

Thrusts pen into DARNLEY'S *hand.*

DARNLEY: Sign?

MORTON: Kneel my lairds! (*They kneel.*) This is a solemn
moment in the history of Scotland.

Still DARNLEY *hesitates.* MARY'S *low laugh comes again. He
turns and looks up at curtain.*

MORTON: They're going to it now my lord—!—Laughing!
Making comparisons!

DARNLEY *whirls back and signs.* LORDS *rise.* MORTON *takes
paper, grunts, satisfied, puts it away. He pushes* DARNLEY *aside as
done with. All draw daggers.*

Right my lords. Quick and quiet.

*In a swift padding rush they are up the steps, tear down the
curtain revealing* MARY *and* RIZZIO.

Signor Rizzio!

He grabs RIZZIO, *throws him to the others. They fall on him like
a pack of dogs. In the uproar.*

MARY: Ho there! Rescue! Treason! Bothwell! Bothwell!

The mangled corpse is let drop. MARY *falls in shock.* DARNLEY
is hanging off, appalled and nerveless. MORTON *angry.*

MORTON: Dagger him man!

DARNLEY *paralyzed. A* LORD *leaps down to him, snatches his
dagger, throws it to* MORTON *who plunges it into the corpse.*

A cry of horror from MARY. BOTHWELL *and* NAU *enter at the
run. Check as* LORDS *present daggers, crouching.* BOTHWELL
spreads his empty hands, approaches and looks at corpse.

BOTHWELL: God's death my lords, you're very thorough. Lord
Darnley, I think this is yours.

Tosses dagger to DARNLEY. *He, piteously:*

DARNLEY: Mary, I—...

He dashes from the stage.

MORTON: Now Lord Bothwell, are you here to hinder or to help?

BOTHWELL: Neither Lord Morton.

MORTON: Then you're in my road.

BOTHWELL: Then may I get out of it?

MORTON: Right out of it Bothwell, out of Edinburgh now.

BOTHWELL: Your Grace. (*She raises her head and looks at him.*) It seems that I must leave you to God's care. I'm for Dunbar. *He goes.*

MORTON: Now Madam, though this was rough yet it was justice.

MARY: No my lord, your pardon, but this was not justice.
She descends unsteadily, NAU hovering anxiously at her side. She crouches at the corpse and sees the wounds.

MARY: Oh God . . .
She rises, bewildered.
He was my friend.

MORTON: He was more than that.

MARY: The fault of that was mine. And I ought to have paid for it. (*She sways, NAU steps to her.*) Claud I was born Queen and have proved carnal. I ought to have been born common! *She reaches for support,* NAU *catching her and lowering her to the ground.* MORTON *gloomy.*

NAU: Good God my lord—What have you done?

MORTON: Our duty. Naething more.
Going. LORDS *following he snarls at them:*
Shift it!

MORTON *and* LORDS *go, dragging corpse.* MARY *watches covertly. When they have gone.*

MARY: Morton, Ruthven, Lindsey, Douglas, Glencairn, Falconside and Kerr—

NAU (*startled*): Madam—?

MARY: Remember them! . . . Remind me every day that they must die.

NAU: Oh Madam this is wild—!—The castle is full of their men! *She looks about. Rises from her knees.*

MARY: So we must quit it.

NAU: There is a guard on every door!

MARY: There will be no guard on the kitchen door. Come.

He follows her, shaken, bewildered.

NAU: But Madam, where?

MARY: Where? To the Border—Dunbar!

They go.

CURTAIN

ACT TWO

The throne is on top of the pyramid now. At the foot of the pyramid stands an ornate golden casket three feet high, with carrying handles. KNOX *in pulpit.* MORTON, RUTHVEN, LINDSEY, *gloomy.*

KNOX: Lord, Lord, what tribulations we have seen. What marching, counter-marching, lying down in the wet heather, rising in the night, what ambushes, what wounds, what death . . . (*Plaintively, descending.*) The execution of the adulterer Rizzio was a very Godly deed, you might have thought that it would prosper. But no, no, Man proposes, God disposes, (*bitterly*) Aye, and the Devil looks after his own. This, an't please you, is a Christening font. Aye—it's no an ornament from a brothel, it's a Christening font. Gurnia, gurnia, solid gold.

VOICE OFF: Ho there, the Queen!

MORTON: Now for God's sake Master Knox, and you must speak, speak small. For our cart has no wheels and the woman's rampant.

  Enter ELIZABETH, WALSINGHAM, LEICESTER, CECIL.

ELIZABETH: Are these the murderers?

KNOX: There was no murder, Madam.

ELIZABETH: What then?

KNOX: Godly execution.

ELIZABETH: I do not think I know a Godly execution. But I know the difference between execution and murder—It is the Royal Warrant.

MORTON: We had it, Madam.

ELIZABETH (*to* WALSINGHAM, *contemptuous*): Darnley's 'warrant'.

KNOX: No Madam, God's.

ELIZABETH: Oh—did he sign it too?

KNOX: That's verra blasph—

ELIZABETH: Peace Master Knox. We are no Edinburgh house-
wife. Morton, how came the Queen to escape?

MORTON: She spoke me fair Madam—God help me, she seemed
(*indignantly*) remorseful.

ELIZABETH: You mean she fooled you.

MORTON: Your Grace the woman is a verra serpent!

ELIZABETH: Poor Adam. Poor, thick-witted, bloody-handed,
Scottish Adam. What do you expect of me?

MORTON: Your mercy, Madam.

KNOX: And your aid Madam.

ELIZABETH: For our mercy, it is universal and you have it. For
our aid: We tell you here before the world, we aid no rebels.
For royalty and rebellion both, are indivisible. Go.

   They go.

Walsingham. Give them money.

WALSINGHAM: Yes Your Grace. How much?

ELIZABETH: As little as will keep them rebellious. Cecil, talk
to Lord Morton.

CECIL: Your Grace.

ELIZABETH: Robin, you have the hardest task.

DUDLEY: Your Grace?

ELIZABETH: Listen to Master Knox. Now—leave us.

   *They go. She approaches the font and looks at it carefully. To
   herself:*

She escapes . . . down little stairs and greasy passages, she
escapes, through the kitchens. I do not know where the
kitchens are . . . And then in the dark, in the sweet smelling
stables, she saddles her own horse; he knows her, he is quiet . . .
I cannot saddle a horse. And then she rides, down rocky screes,
through mountain rivers, two days and nights two hundred
miles, she must have ridden without sleep . . . And *I* am
sleepless I am spent. And then, this Bothwell—raises men,
half-naked men whose whole wealth is a sword and drives

her enemies from Edinburgh—and for what? Why, for herself . . . And now she returns, but easily now, easily. (*Harsh.*)
For she is big with child. And that child is my heir, for I am
a barren stock!

She ascends to throne as MARY, LADIES, BOTHWELL,
ARCHBISHOP, MOR *and* NAU *enter.* MARY *carrying a baby. She
goes to the font.* ELIZABETH *calls:*

Your Grace—Your rebel subjects came here and appealed to
us. But we have given them a sour reply. And for a further
token of our love, we send you this.

MARY: Your Grace, we guess what manner of reply you gave
our rebel subjects. Your Grace may guess our gratitude. And
for this further token of your love—Why, we will put it to
good use!

ARCHBISHOP *dips into font and:*

ARCHBISHOP: In the name of the Father, Son, and Holy Ghost:
James Stuart, Prince of Scotland, Ireland, and England!

Fanfare.

ELIZABETH *exits above.*

MARY *takes the child, peering at it delightedly, taking it back
towards* BOTHWELL, *softly:*

MARY: Hey boy, shall we ride? Hey? Shall we ride together you
and I—Hey boy? Shall we then—?—Oh! (*She laughs up at*
BOTHWELL.) *He sneezed.*

BOTHWELL *nods coldly and:*

BOTHWELL: He's very talented, no doubt about it.

MARY *smiles, says again to the baby:*

MARY: And so he is. No doubt about it.

NAU: Your Grace must now appoint the Lord Protector.

BOTHWELL: The job is spoken for.

MARY: What needs he with a Lord Protector? He will make
shift with a Queen Protector—Won't you boy, hey?

NAU: Madam, these are not the times to break an ancient custom;
beseech you to decide upon some valiant and sober gentleman
who—

BOTHWELL: Are you deaf man—?—The job's spoken for.

MARY *looks at* BOTHWELL *thoughtfully, a little sadly, down again at the baby and softly:*

MARY: Lord Mor.

MOR *steps forward.* BOTHWELL *watches darkly.*

Lord Mor, I give into your guard this most precious burden.

MOR: It is a trust that I will answer for to God himself Your Grace.

MARY (*smiling, ready to weep, relinquishing the baby*): Thanks my lord.

MOR *goes with baby,* LADIES *following.* MARY'S *eyes and body yearn after them and:*

Bring him to me ladies before supper!

All go except MARY *and* BOTHWELL.

BOTHWELL (*quietly*): So you don't trust me.

MARY (*frightened, placating*): With myself I trust you.

Looking away from her, gloomily grunts.

BOTHWELL: Mebbe.

MARY: I have no choice but trust you, being your slave.

BOTHWELL: Don't you know yourself better than that? You're nobody's slave.

MARY: It is you who do not know me. See.

She goes down, clasping his legs, abased.

BOTHWELL: That's just extravagance. Let go my legs. You want it both ways, Mary. Like—you'll feed me food on a fork. But I must eat it whether I've a mind to it or not, or you'll sling the plate across the room. You've a bluidy awful temper, d'you know that?

MARY: Yes.

BOTHWELL: An you were my wife, I'd have taken a whip to you before this.

MARY: Well, I would be your wife in anything I can.

She smiles up sideways and catlike, but he leaves her; soberly:

BOTHWELL: I doubt that. With me to your bed here in Edinburgh, and Darnley to your husband away there in Glasgow, you have it both ways, the way you want it. I doubt you'd be my wife.

MARY: I have given you no cause to doubt it.

BOTHWELL: There's an easy way to prove it. Fetch him here.

She rises, wretched, looks away.

He, sadly, bitterly:

You're playing, Mary. You play at everything. You think that life's a game and you the only one allowed to cheat. Well it's no a game and you canna cheat, for there are no rules. It's real. But you're no a real woman.

MARY: You lie.

BOTHWELL: Yes I lie. Come here.

She goes to him. He kisses her, quite gently. Her response becomes fierce. Deliberately, he holds her away and:

Do you fetch him?

She searches his face.

MARY: Jamie; do you know what you are asking?

BOTHWELL: Yes; everything. Ought I to ask for less?

MARY: I'll fetch him.

She goes. BOTHWELL *calls:*

BOTHWELL: Ormiston!

ORMISTON *enters, peeling an apple.*

Well?

ORMISTON: Well . . . I have forty-five pounds of it; in three wee kegs. It should suffice.

BOTHWELL: To Hell with should; will it?

ORMISTON: It's no just the verra best powder I've seen; it has a sort of greyish look, guid powder's black. And Kirk o' Field's a gey strong house. Aye, strongly built. What like did you want with the house?

BOTHWELL: I want it lifted off the earth.

ORMISTON: Forty-five pounds'll no do that.

BOTHWELL: Get more then.

ORMISTON: That's a' verra well. It's not easy come by, not

quietly. And there's enough folk ken what you're about already.

BOTHWELL: Who?

ORMISTON: That's hard to say. But since she went to Glasgow there's been a sort of gathering in the air. Have you not noticed?

BOTHWELL: Yes.

TALA enters with letter. Gives it to BOTHWELL.

TALA: A letter laird, from herself in Glasgow.

BOTHWELL: How is it?

TALA: You're in deep water I would say. He's awfu' sick. She's sorry for him.

BOTHWELL: Hell.

He opens the letter and reads. The two men look over his shoulder.

ORMISTON: It's a guid hand is that.

TALA: It's a French hand.

ORMISTON: Is that right?

BOTHWELL: Off you dogs!

He reads:

'Being absent from him who has my heart—' mp.

Turns several pages impatiently.

TALA: It's a long letter.

ORMISTON: Why wouldn't it be? It's a love letter.

BOTHWELL: 'His sickness abates yet he has almost slain me with his breath though I came no nearer than the bed's foot. For Rizzio he says—' Curse what he says, is he coming? 'Alas my lord—' (*Impatient growl, another page.*) 'I cannot sleep because I cannot sleep . . .' Hell and Damnation is he coming or not? 'Summa. He will not come except— . . . And so I have promised. We come—

He turns a page. Breathes out, satisfied:

to-morrow . . .' Ormiston, how much to make it certain?

ORMISTON: Another hundred pounds.

BOTHWELL: Get it from the armoury.

Throws a ring of keys which ORMISTON *catches and, dangling them, dubiously.*

ORMISTON: It's awfu' obvious.

BOTHWELL (*scanning letter again*): Do it.

ORMISTON: You're the master; I'm the man.

He goes, with TALA. BOTHWELL *reads again:*

BOTHWELL: 'It is late, I am alone, I desire never to cease writing, yet now must cease for lack of paper and so end my letter. Read it twice or thrice. Burn it.' Burn it? Oh no, my love; this is my warrant.

MARY *enters above. She is alone.*

Fierce:

Where is he? Have you not fetched him?

MARY: Yes. Jamie, what do you mean to do?

He looks at her hard.

BOTHWELL: Don't ask what I will do. You've done your part.

DARNLEY *and* DOCTOR *enter above.* DARNLEY *wears a weird white mask, white gloves and slippers, a fanciful white dressing gown.*

DARNLEY: Mary—

BOTHWELL *turns and stares.*

BOTHWELL: What—?

MARY: Jamie—He is defaced.

BOTHWELL: Defaced—?—Why it's only a touch of the pox my Lord. Let's have a look—

MARY: Leave him alone, Jamie!

He turns and stares at her grimly.

DARNLEY: Bothwell—The Queen and I are reconciled.

BOTHWELL: Yes I see you are . . . (*Turns back to* DARNLEY *cheerful.*) And I'm very glad of it, my Lord. I have your room prepared at Kirk o' Field.

DARNLEY: What, am I not for the castle?

BOTHWELL: The Doctors say the air at Kirk o' Fields is healthier. Is that not right, Doctor?

DOCTOR: The air at Kirk o' Fields, Lord Bothwell, is humorous, the place being—

BOTHWELL: —My Doctor says its healthier. (*Cheerful again to* DARNLEY.) And we've everything made ready there. But we can shift you to the castle in the morning if you like.

During this MARY, *staring at* BOTHWELL *has come to stand protectively near* DARNLEY, *behind his chair.*

DARNLEY: Well . . . (*To* MARY.) Will you come with me?

MARY (*looking over his head at* BOTHWELL *defiantly*): Yes.

BOTHWELL: Well you cannot go tonight Your Grace. The Dance is tonight.

MARY: The dance?

BOTHWELL: Your guid friend Bastien's—

Unseen by DARNLEY *he jabs his thumb at his own chest, identifying 'Bastien'—*

wedding dance.

MARY: I will excuse myself.

BOTHWELL: Well you can do that if you like—But I fancy it's the last you'll see of Bastien, if you do.

MARY (*dully*): I will come to you Harry, after the dance.

BOTHWELL: Kirk o' Fields Doctor! Good-night my lord.

DARNLEY (*going*): Mary . . .?

MARY: I will come to you Harry, after the dance!

DARNLEY *and* DOCTOR *gone.*

Dully again:

Is it tonight?

BOTHWELL: Is what tonight?

MARY: I do not know.

BOTHWELL (*gently*): That's right. So dance.

MUSIC. *He takes her hand. They dance the Pavane. Lights fade. Shadowy figures enter behind, dancing two by two.* MARY *in bright spot, puppetlike under* BOTHWELL'S *compelling stare. He leaves her. She makes an involuntary gesture to retain him. Then dances on alone, her face frightened.* MUSIC *ceases. A solitary drum taps out the time. Then on Speakers a Child's Voice:*

CHILD'S VOICE (*speaker*): 'Mary, Mary, quite contrary, how

does your garden grow? With silver bells and cockle shells and pretty maids—'

The stage rocks in blinding light. A distant explosion bellows. Uproar, Dancers scattering, bells and crowd roaring on Speaker. KNOX dashes on, beside himself, stands in the spot vacated by MARY.

KNOX: Did I not warn you? Did I not say? Did I not prophesy? Was not the very face of Heaven dark the day she set her foot on Scottish soil?

Lights up. The Dancers revealed as ELIZABETH, WALSINGHAM, CECIL; LADIES, DE QUADRA, PHILIP; POPE and PRIEST. The SCOTS LORDS are on the lowest step of pyramid, looking up like everybody else at MARY seated on throne, BOTHWELL by her, both composed but desperately tense.

How long guid people of Edinburgh—how long? Are you God's children and the nurslings of the Kirk and will you have a bloody handed strumpet for your Queen?

MARY: John Knox—you are a traitor and a—

BOTHWELL: —Hold hard, the world is watching you.

MARY: Good Master Knox, we have no quarrel with you—or our people.

KNOX: By Heaven we have a quarrel with you!

ELIZABETH: Your Grace, we should not do the office of a cousin and a friend unless we urged Your Grace to clear yourself. Repudiate that man—bring him to trial!

MARY: We thank Your Grace, but this gentleman has stood his trial and is found innocent.

KNOX: We know the manner of that trial, and if he's innocent, why so is Satan!

MARY: The law stands over all of us, and we think as the law does, that the gentleman is innocent. In proof of which know all the world that we are married.

KNOX: That does not prove his innocence—it indicates your guilt!

POPE: A Protestant pantomime my child, no marriage. Repudiate him.

MARY: Your Holiness, although the form was empty yet our hearts were in it; I account us married in the eyes of God.

PHILIP: Poor fool, poor *fool*!

KNOX: Oh my what sympathy these Catholics show for their own kind. The King of Spain now. Thinks himself a verra pious man. The ladies of his Court must dress just so, no hanky-panky in the Prado no, a verra nunnery they say. Well here we have adultery, and bigamy, and murder—! And what says His pious Majesty? Why not a word.

PHILIP: We nothing doubt but that the lady was involved against her will and merits leniency.

KNOX: The woman is a common criminal and merits death.

The Dancers wheel, look up at MARY, *go.*

MARY: Lord Mor—Give me my child.

She half descends to meet MOR *who moves to meet her, but* MORTON:

MORTON: Give her the child, you give it to Lord Bothwell, Mor. Is that how you'll discharge your trust?

MOR hesitates.

MARY: Lord Mor—!

MOR: I cannot, Madam, while that man is by your side.

MORTON: So let us have Lord Bothwell and you can have your child.

MARY: What mean you with Lord Bothwell?

MORTON: We mean to hang him.

MARY (*kisses her fingertips and tenderly extends her arm towards her child*): Farewell, child . . .

MOR goes and she watches him off. BOTHWELL *grins at* MORTON.

MORTON: You're makin' it hard for us Your Grace, but you're makin' it gey harder for yourself. To me, Bothwell. (*He and* LORDS *draw their daggers.*)

BOTHWELL: Ormiston!

MORTON: We've hanged him already.

BOTHWELL: Tala! Bowton! A Hepburn! A Hepburn!

MORTON: You're wasting your breath man—you have a sort
of plague. Are you coming down or must we come up?

    BOTHWELL *draws his dagger.* MORTON *sighs.*

Verra well my lords—Quick and quiet.

    LORDS *start for the steps.*

MARY: Stop!

    They stop.

Lord Morton, if I submit myself to you, will you let Lord
Bothwell go?

MORTON (*considers, nods, pleased*): . . . Done.

    LORDS *protest.*

Peace you fools. What's one Border Bandit more or less?
Bothwell you have three days to quit Scotland.

MARY: Go Jamie.

    He kisses her, is going.

Be true!

BOTHWELL: I only met one woman in my life; d'you think I'll
no come back for her?

    He goes. She looking after him, radiant. Turns to MORTON,

MARY: Now may you do your worst Lord Morton.

MORTON: Well I ask myself what I am to do with you.

    His tone is quite friendly, and KNOX, *alert and threatening:*

KNOX: Morton, will you parley with this harlot?

MORTON: I will John. Yes.

KNOX: Then I will go and parley with the People!

    They measure glances.

MORTON: You do that, John.

    He watches KNOX *exit then sighs.*

Gurnia, gurnia, troubled times . . . The way of it Your Grace
is this: We cannot and we will not have Lord Bothwell for
our King. You must see that? But neither would we have the
People for our King. A Queen you see is a great convenience
to the nobility—And vicky versa. Now, you're not tied to
Bothwell very hard. The way I see it, that marriage was no
marriage. Because, the way I see it, you was forced. So you

see Your Grace, if you'll just say that you was forced,
repudiate the man, why then, we're all in step again.

MARY: And what if I refuse?

MORTON: Now what would you gain by that? He'll no come
back.

MARY: He will come back.

MORTON: If he comes back we'll put him to the horn and hunt
him down like any other outlaw and he knows it. There's no
'Chivalry' in Bothwell.

MARY: Still you have not told me what, if I refuse.

MORTON: Prison. And I do not mean 'confinement' in some
bra' house, no no—I mean a Highland keep. I mean one small,
strong, room, for the rest of your days. And you're young yet.

MARY: And that is my choice?

MORTON: It is, d'you want time to think?

MARY: No. For prison, I will quit it. And then woe to you;
woe to this country. For Lord Bothwell . . .
    Her level voice falters on it. Then strongly.
My lords I would follow him to the edge of the earth—in my
shift!

MORTON (*angry*): . . . You obdurate shrew. Awa' wi' her!
    He shoves her into their arms. They run her off stage, MORTON
    looking after. Light change. Enter ELIZABETH, WALSINGHAM,
    CECIL.

ELIZABETH: To the edge of the earth . . .?

MORTON: Aye Your Grace. In her shift.

ELIZABETH: . . . Well . . . Where is she?

MORTON (*complacent*): We have her fast. (*Grim satisfaction.*) At
Loch Leven.

ELIZABETH: What is that?

MORTON: A Highland keep, Your Grace; the keep on an island,
the island in a lake.

ELIZABETH: Her jailer?

MORTON (*chuckle*): Dinna fash about that, Your Grace. He'd as
soon break her neck as look at her. Black Douglas is his name.

ELIZABETH: Who has the child?

MORTON (*sour smile*): One George Buchanann, a verra Godly friend of Master Knox.

ELIZABETH (*nods*): Will the Queen see the child?

MORTON: She will not.

ELIZABETH: Well. Rule Scotland wisely Morton, till the little King grows up.

> *She pushes a bag of coins across the table.* MORTON, *unctuously:*

MORTON: I will rule as Your Grace would wish.

> *Enter* DAVISON.

DAVISON: Your pardon Your Grace. Master Cecil this presses. (*Gives letter to* CECIL.) From the Border, Your Grace. It concerns Lord Morton somewhat.

MORTON: Me?

CECIL (*eyes on the paper*): Yes . . . Yes, rather more than somewhat. The Queen of Scots is free Your Grace.

ELIZABETH: Free?

CECIL: Yes Your Grace, it—

MORTON: I dinna believe it!

CECIL (*still scanning paper*): It would appear that your mysoginistic friend Black Douglas has a son, of a more impressionable temper.

MORTON: What—! (*Snatches letter and peruses it, breathing hard.*)

> ELIZABETH *laughs suddenly.* CECIL *goes on:*

CECIL: And the keep had a window. And the lake had a boat.

> ELIZABETH *laughs again.* MORTON *looks up.*

MORTON: What Madam, are you merry?

ELIZABETH: All men are merry for a moment, Morton, to see a bird go free. There, my merriment is over.

MORTON: I think so Madam. She is in England.

CECIL: What?

MORTON (*cheerfully*): Aye—She's in Carlisle, Master Cecil, lodged with the Earl of Westmorland—

WALSINGHAM (*alarmed, to* CECIL):—Westmorland!

MORTON: Aye—And other Catholic gentlemen are flocking

there—'flocking' that's the word here. To cap it a', she throws herself on Your Grace's mercy and (*throws down the letter*) asks audience.

ELIZABETH *picks up the letter and stares at it. Then, almost to herself, in a voice almost of dread:*

ELIZABETH: Why me . . .? Why my mercy . . .? We are enemies.

CECIL *is watching her carefully; now, carefully:*

CECIL: If you see her, Your Grace, you will seem to condone the murder of Lord Darnley.

WALSINGHAM: That woman alive in England is a Trojan Horse. Execute her!

ELIZABETH: It would not be seen as the execution of a murderess, good Francis, it would be seen as the elimination of a rival.

CECIL: Yes . . . It would *be* the elimination of a rival of course.

ELIZABETH: No.

CECIL: I wonder if the matter is not Scottish domestic . . .

ELIZABETH: Good . . . (*Smiling.*) Lord Morton you make take our sister back to Scotland and (*Smile goes flat and expressionless.*) do with her what you will.

MORTON (*reproving grin*): Oh no Your Grace. She's yours. An' Your Grace is welcome. (*Takes money, going.*) Where she is, there is no safety.

He goes. They look after him.

WALSINGHAM: There is no safety for Your Grace's person *while* she is. She has connived at murder once and will again.

CECIL: I would that we had proof that she connived at it.

WALSINGHAM: I have a letter here, would hang her in a common court. She wrote it from Glasgow. It was taken from among Lord Bothwell's papers.

ELIZABETH *takes it; is troubled; thrusts it at* CECIL *who takes it eagerly and then asks with mild curiosity.*

CECIL: Is it genuine Master Walsingham or forged?

WALSINGHAM: Read it.

ELIZABETH: Aloud.

CECIL (*reads*): 'Being absent from the place where I left my heart, I was like a body without a heart—'

ELIZABETH shifts fractionally. CECIL *registers it, says to* WALSINGHAM.

Poetic; hardly proof.

WALSINGHAM: Read the portions I have marked.

CECIL (*reads*): 'Alas my lord, you have sent me here to do a work I much detest . . .' er '. . . Certainly he fears the thing you know of and for his life. But I had but to speak two or three kind words and he was happy. Then he showed so many little courtesies so seriously and wisely that you would be amazed. Alas, alas, and I never deceived anybody . . .' er 'It is late and yet I cannot sleep because I cannot sleep as I desire, that is in your arms my dear life . . .'

She shifts again. He stops, lays down the letter.

More of the like.

ELIZABETH: Finish it.

CECIL: Madam the rest is—(*Waves the rest away.*)

ELIZABETH: Finish it.

He picks it up and reads the rest in a tone which tries to drain it of emotion and therefore heightens it:

CECIL: 'Now God forgive me and God give you my only love the fortune which your humble faithful love desires for you. It is late. I am alone. I desire never to cease writing to you, yet now must cease for lack of paper. And so I kiss your hands and end my letter. Read it twice or thrice. Burn it.'

He lays it down, and waits for her response. It comes flatly:

ELIZABETH: And he kept it.

WALSINGHAM: Happily Madam, yes.

ELIZABETH: Well that is no forgery. (*She rises, not looking at them.*) Send sufficient force and bring her as far South as Sheffield Castle. Confine her there. But as a Queen.

WALSINGHAM: She may correspond?

ELIZABETH: She may do anything a Queen may do. Except leave Sheffield Castle.

WALSINGHAM: It is not wise Your Grace.

ELIZABETH: It is our will! (*Turns at exit to say unconvincingly.*)
We fear the French connection.

She goes. WALSINGHAM *severe:*

WALSINGHAM: Her Grace is too merciful!

CECIL: I do not think that this is altogether mercy. I think our
Queen sees Mary in the mirror.

WALSINGHAM: You are grown so subtle Master Cecil you will
shortly be invisible.

He goes, impatient, CECIL *following. Light change. Enter
separately,* NAU *and* SERVANT *who puts down a small keg.*

SERVANT: There sir, from Lord Shrewsbury's own hopyards.
The best beer in England.

NAU: Lord Shrewsbury is a kindly jailor. Thank him.

SERVANT goes. MARY *enters slowly, in a simple riding habit,
carrying a whip.*

Where did you ride Your Grace?

MARY: To the North Gate Claud.

She somnambulates past him. Stops.

And then to the West Gate . . . And so to the South Gate . . .
And back to the Castle.

NAU: Are you unwell?

MARY: I am in the best health possible, for prison. This morning
I am cured of hope.

NAU: Madam?

MARY: I met a person in the Park. A Catholic gentleman. He
said 'God Bless Your Grace'. And gave me news of my lord
Bothwell. He will not come back Claud. He is in Denmark.

NAU: Perhaps he waits his time, Your Grace.

MARY: He has taken service with the King of Denmark.

NAU: He must provide for himself somehow.

MARY: He has bought a house.

NAU: He must have a roof.

MARY: There is a lady in the house.

NAU: How did the gentleman know all this?

MARY: He has seen it.

NAU *has no answer, looks at her in pity. She gives him a pale smile.*

He only told me what you told me long ago. And what my own heart has been heavy with these twelve slow months. I think the months will seem to pass more swiftly now. (*She looks at him.*) Claud, I do not ask that you should share them.

NAU: An't please Your Grace, I will share them.

MARY: Henceforth you are the only man that I will trust. (*Bitter self-recrimination.*) Besides the man I ought to have staked my life on from the start.

NAU: What man is that Your Grace?

MARY: The little man in Scotland, Claud.

NAU: It is cruel that they do not let you see him.

MARY: I see him every night. We talk before we sleep.

NAU: What does he say?

MARY: That he loves me right well. And forgives me . . . And, that when he is of age, he will come out of Scotland like a second Tamurlaine—!—With bloody punishment in either hand for these water hearted, beerdrinkers!

NAU: Oh Madam be patient!

MARY: Well, I will.

NAU: You must Your Grace!

MARY: I must.

She has made a swift tour of the stage, mindless as an animal and comes now to a halt with her whip flicking restlessly. NAU *looks at her uneasily; a silence, then, indicating the keg at his feet he offers:*

NAU (*cheerfully*): Myself, I have learned to *like* the beer.

MARY: It is an accomplishment.

The whip flicks again. He eyes her again.

NAU: Show patient, Madam, and the English may at length show kind.

MARY: By God, they'll show unlike themselves then.

NAU: There is kindness in the circumstances they allow you

here. And Mignon, you would need less patience if you would make more use of them.

MARY: I use the Park. (*She shows him the whip.*)

NAU: Your riding to and fro like one demented half the day serves but to remind you that the Park has walls. There is a wide world in the library.

MARY: I'll come more often to the library.

NAU: There are some fine romances there.

MARY (*a pause*): I have done with romances. (*A pause.*) Henceforth I'll study policy.

NAU: Patience now is your only policy.

MARY: No.

NAU: What other?

MARY: Claud, this gentleman whom I met riding in the Park. He will carry letters, secret letters, they will not be overlooked.

NAU: Oh no—!

MARY: He is waiting for me now.

NAU: Waiting for—?—Oh Madam, Madam—What do you know of this gentleman—?—Think! Your life lies every morning in the Queen of England's hand.

MARY: She does not dare.

NAU: And if you give her just occasion she will dare! Be patient! and *preserve* yourself!

　　She considers it. Then, reasonably, quietly:

MARY: For what?

NAU: For quietness. Your Grace, you have some need of quietness. In quietness we save our souls.

MARY: Sir, do you think I do not know, what state my soul is in . . .?

　　It rebukes him.

But listen now. God gives each one of us a different life to live. And if we live it well he gives us everlasting life in Heaven. And if we live it ill, as surely I have lived right ill, yet still may Heaven be merciful. But if we live it not at all nay then I think Heaven has no mercy—And God made me a

Queen! I did not beg to be so born. And maybe I was not equipped to be so born. But since I was so born—(*She collects herself.*)—By Heaven I will so live!

She goes where she entered, but striding fast. NAU *separately. An echoing cry of anguish, off:*

VOICE OFF: No—no—no—no—! (*A pause.*) Oh God—!—Help me!

PRISONER *dragged into spot by* JAILERS. CECIL *and* WALSINGHAM *enter as lights come up.*

They do not look. WALSINGHAM *sits.* CECIL *addresses audience.*

CECIL: The Pope of Rome is a dangerous simpleton. And he has had letters from the Queen of Scots which I fear dangerously misrepresent the situation here. For here I have his Papal edict 'Regnan in Excelsis' which releases English Catholics from allegiance to the Queen. Nay more—It makes it meritorious in English Catholics to assassinate the Queen. And more again—It calls for a crusade to invade the territories of the Queen. So now our English Catholics have to choose, between his Holiness and her Majesty. Well His Holiness is far away and Her Majesty is close at hand and we her Ministers are (*half glance at* PRISONER) busy. How would you choose? Yes and so do most of they. Not all though . . . No, not all. (*He joins* WALSINGHAM *at table.*) Well I see that you have racked him.

JAILER: Yes sir.

CECIL: Can he stand?

JAILER: No sir.

CECIL: A chair then.

PRISONER *seated.* CECIL *looks at him unwillingly. His silvery old man's voice is courteous, dispassionate and fatal:*

CECIL: Now sir again, who are you?

PRISONER: I am Nicholas Benson. Cloth Merchant, of Amsterdam.

CECIL: No sir. You are—

V.V.R.—4*

WALSINGHAM *gives him paper.*

—Father Edward Fenton and you are a Jesuit priest. You were trained at Douai and sent here from there. While you were in prison at Norwich you administered the Sacrament of 'absolution' to a man you took to be a fellow prisoner awaiting death. And you told him all this. One Peter Blunt.

PRISONER: Oh . . . Was Peter not a prisoner?

CECIL: No. he was an instrument of Master Walsingham's.

PRISONER: Oh. (*Without much feeling.*) I am undone then.

CECIL: Yes. Now, your letters—(*Reaching for them.*)

PRISONER: They are not my letters.

CECIL: The letters which were found beneath the floorboards of your room. They implicate you in a plot, which we already know about. (*Gently, pleadingly.*) We know about it, sir.

PRISONER: What need to question then?

CECIL: I should like to understand you if I could. Did you know that your associates intended to assassinate Her Majesty?

No answer.

Did you know that following that, one hundred Catholic gentlemen would seize the port of Norwich while two thousand Spanish troops were landed there—on English soil?

WALSINGHAM: To make that bloody-handed harlot Mary Stuart, England's Queen? And do you call this a Crusade? And yourself English?

PRISONER: God made Mary Stuart England's Queen. It is not for me—or you—to question it.

WALSINGHAM: Ho! 'God' quotha! Lackaday what Christianity is this!

CECIL: Walsingham. Look sir, you know that you must die—

PRISONER: I do; and God be thanked am ready to.

CECIL: I see you are. But you can die by burning, as a priest. Or, for treason, quickly by the axe. That choice I can give you . . . Now. I want to know if Mary Stuart instigated, or approved, or knew about your plans . . . Sir I have seen death by burning, in Mary Tudor's time. I know which I would choose.

PRISONER (*smiles faintly*): But then I have a higher calling than yourself. I am a priest. And I will die as one.

A beat.

Then CECIL *motions with his hand and* JAILERS *remove* PRISONER. CECIL'S *face is pinched and wrinkled with distaste. He tells the audience:*

CECIL: One grows old quickly at this work.

ELIZABETH *enters. She too is older than before. Her face, framed in an extravagantly flaring collar, is more obviously painted. She growls suspiciously at* CECIL.

ELIZABETH: What do you say, Cecil?

CECIL: That I am growing old Your Grace. It is only Your Grace who has the secret of eternal youth, and shines on like the morning star when all the rest have fled, a rainbow among clouds, a rose in Winter.

ELIZABETH: Leave flattery to courtiers. You give good measure but the quality is coarse. Well; what have you found?

WALSINGHAM: We have found the same as always Madam: Mary Stuart. Mary Stuart and Catholic Conspiracy, Mary Stuart and a Spanish rescue, Mary Stuart and Your Grace's death. Your Grace was to have been shot down with muskets in the knot garden at Hampton Court, on Tuesday next.

ELIZABETH: Muskets? In the knot garden . . .? God's death, how long does this go on?

WALSINGHAM: As long as Mary Stuart lives Your Grace.

ELIZABETH: Have you proof of her complicity?

WALSINGHAM: No proof, Your Grace, but no doubt either.

ELIZABETH: I will not do it without proof.

She says it stubbornly, as something said before, and WALSINGHAM *looks at* CECIL *who:*

CECIL: Your Grace there is news from Spain. The Duke of Parma is appointed to command the Spanish armies in the Netherlands.

Enter DAVISON.

DAVISON: Your Grace, the Spanish Ambassador asks instant audience.

ELIZABETH: Tomorrow.

Exit DAVISON.

Parma for the Netherlands.

CECIL: Yes Your Grace. He will be followed by fifty thousand infantry.

ELIZABETH: Oh . . . This is not for the Netherlands.

WALSINGHAM: No Your Grace it is for us. And it will find the country in two minds—because it has two Queens!

ELIZABETH: I cannot do it without proof!

WALSINGHAM *goes. She rises: energy beginning to flow from her visibly.*

Yet, Parma. Something I must do.

CECIL: Yes Your Grace.

ELIZABETH: What?

CECIL: May I speak without fear?

ELIZABETH: I do not know that; you may speak.

CECIL: Recall the Earl of Leicester.

ELIZABETH: Nay, you had done better to be silent.

CECIL: Your Grace he is a soldier.

ELIZABETH: I have other soldiers.

CECIL: But none so fit.

ELIZABETH: Fit—? And he were Hannibal he were not fit— He is treacherous!

CECIL: Madam, marriage is not treachery.

ELIZABETH: But secrecy is treachery! Speak no more of Leicester, he is ruined! What—Ten months the slippery villain plays it out with 'Yes Your Grace' and 'No Your Grace' and then 'A trifle I would tell Your Grace—I am married these ten months'! Speak not Cecil—!—I will not hear!

CECIL: Or let me speak or let me go, Your Grace.

ELIZABETH: Nay, go then.

He goes.

Come back.
He comes back.
Suffolk?

CECIL: Too old Your Grace.

ELIZABETH: Mountjoy?

CECIL: Too young.
She goes to throne, calls formally:

ELIZABETH: Recall the Earl—of Leicester!
Enter DAVISON and DUDLEY, also older than before.
My lord.
He kisses her hand and rises.
Are you well?

DUDLEY: Well indeed Your Grace. Now.

ELIZABETH: And your wife?

DUDLEY: Well too, Your Grace.

ELIZABETH: You are happy?

DUDLEY: I am a husband, Madam.

ELIZABETH: You make it sound little. What more would you be?
She is looking away. DUDLEY *snatches a look at* CECIL, *who nods.*

DUDLEY: Your Grace—this summer—I hope to be a father.
She looks at him. Moves; right past him to table.

ELIZABETH: Take your place my lord.

CECIL: My lord is acquainted with the occasion.
She returns from her abstraction.

ELIZABETH: Oh yes the occasion. What do you think?

DUDLEY: I think we might shock them, if we had time to muster, and if the country were united.

ELIZABETH: . . . And what do you think might unite the country?

DUDLEY: The death of Mary Stuart.

ELIZABETH (*softly*): By God, time was you had other plans for Mary Stuart.

DUDLEY (*uncomfortable*): Time has changed Your Grace.

ELIZABETH: And you with it. I hope you will prove a constant soldier Robin; for Heaven knows you're an unsteady swain.
Silence. She throws it off. Brisk:
How long to muster?

DUDLEY: Three to muster, three to train.

ELIZABETH: Six months in all. And Parma's veterans have not been out of iron for sixteen years—And he will shock them. Cecil, this fifty thousand—will they come overland?
She sits bolt upright and expressionless during what follows, a political computer gathering information.

CECIL: They will if France will let them through, Your Grace.

ELIZABETH: And will France let them through?

CECIL: Not if Your Grace will make the French alliance.

ELIZABETH: Meaning the French marriage.

CECIL: Yes Your Grace.

ELIZABETH: Walsingham, has Spain sufficient ships to carry fifty thousand?

WALSINGHAM: Your Grace, there is such hammering in the Spanish shipyards that Spain shakes.

ELIZABETH: Have we sufficient ships to sink them?

CECIL: Not yet Your Grace.

ELIZABETH: And you require six months to muster.

DUDLEY: Yes Your Grace.
CLERK enters.

CLERK: Signor de Quadra, as Your Grace appointed yesterday, asks audience again today.

ELIZABETH: Again tomorrow.
CLERK goes. She turns to DAVISON.
You sir, tell the French Prince we will have him.
DAVISON goes.

WALSINGHAM: He is a Catholic Your Grace, your people will not have him.

ELIZABETH: Nor will we; so send a hundred thousand crowns to him, to keep his relish for our person keen.
WALSINGHAM goes, while CECIL gasps:

CECIL: A hundred thousand crowns Your Grace!

ELIZABETH: Our person needs a little spice. Sell Crown lands to the value of two hundred thousand.

CECIL: Madam—Sell Crown land?

ELIZABETH: There is a time when thrift becomes extravagant old man and this is such a time. The other hundred thousand send to Plymouth. Sir Francis Drake will tell you it will build six ships, tell him it must build me ten. If he must use green timber, so. These ships must float till Parma's great Armada comes, thereafter they may sink for me. You sir—

    CECIL going but stops enthralled to see the last of the firework display.

Raise volunteers and send them to the Netherlands to occupy the Duke of Parma there awhile.

DUDLEY: Yes Your Grace.

ELIZABETH: And muster.

DUDLEY: Yes Your Grace.

ELIZABETH: And train.

DUDLEY: Yes Your Grace.

ELIZABETH: And Robin—

DUDLEY: Yes Your Grace?

ELIZABETH: I am glad to see you.

    DUDLEY goes.

CECIL: Madam.

ELIZABETH: What?

CECIL: You are a greater monarch than your father.

    She looks at him.

And he was a man among men Your Grace.

ELIZABETH: Our very thought.

    He goes. Perfect stillness for a second. Her face remains rigid but her body crumples; she is exhausted. DAVISON *enters.*

DAVISON: Your Grace, Signor de Quadra demands instant audience.

ELIZABETH (*revivified*): Nay and he demands it, let him have it.

    DAVISON *goes; she descends.*

DE QUADRA *enters.*

DE QUADRA: How now Your Grace—!

ELIZABETH: How now de Quadra, where have you been?

DE QUADRA: Been—? This fortnight I have been outside Your
Grace's door—with heavy business for Your Grace.

ELIZABETH: Oh would that I had known; this fortnight I have
been so idle that the hours have seemed like fortnights.

DE QUADRA: By Heaven Your Grace—Your shipbuilders aren't
idle!

ELIZABETH (*as accepting a compliment upon her people's industry*):
Are they not? Oh good. Nothing so conduces to the welfare
of the State as an industrious artisan.

DE QUADRA: My master would know what your shipbuilders do!

ELIZABETH: Well sir I am not familiar with that business, but
I take it they build ships.

DE QUADRA: For what?

ELIZABETH: Why to go a-sailing in.

DE QUADRA: Well certainly Your Grace's talk is idle.
    She blinks, but then:

ELIZABETH. Then let us talk of something else.

DE QUADRA: I am to ask Your Grace why there are suddenly a
thousand English volunteers who fight against my master in
the Netherlands.

ELIZABETH: Fashion, de Quadra, simply fashion. Our young
men like to say that they have fought against the Duke of
Parma as their silly sisters like to say that they have fetched
their ruffs from Paris.

DE QUADRA: I hear Your Grace has sent a hundred thousand
crowns to Paris—from your privy purse!

ELIZABETH (*a little pause and then*): For ruffs.

DE QUADRA: Your Grace, if you will make no weightier replies
to these my master's just complaints I fear lest the amity
between yourself and him may wither, and enmity ensue.

ELIZABETH: Are you instructed to say this?

DE QUADRA: Yes Your Grace.

ELIZABETH: I'm sorry. (*Calls.*) Walsingham!

WALSINGHAM enters, with another of the dossiers, which he places on the table.

Walsingham, the King of Spain complains that we make ready to defend ourselves against his Great Armada. This gentleman complains that I make light replies. Furnish him with something heavier.

WALSINGHAM: Well sir, this is something heavy.

He dumps into DE QUADRA's arms the topmost of the piled dossiers. DE QUADRA raises his eyebrows.

DE QUADRA: Heavy yes; what else is it?

WALSINGHAM: That sir, is the evidence concerning Father Edward Fenton, who conspired to assassinate Her Majesty and proclaim Mary Stuart in her place—by Spanish force of arms.

DE QUADRA: I know no Father Fenton.

He is about to put back the dossier but WALSINGHAM whips another on top of it.

WALSINGHAM: Nor Thomas Throgmorton?

DE QUADRA: Nor Thomas Throgmorton.

WALSINGHAM: Ha! Nor Roberto Ridolfi, I suppose—? Nor Henry Cockeyn, nor George Douglas, nor George Gifford, Creighton, Paget, Parsons, Holt?

He reels off the list of hated names, dumping dossiers in DE QUADRA's arms the while DE QUADRA can barely see above them, but he keeps his dignity. Flatly:

DE QUADRA: No.

WALSINGHAM: Now that is strange, for they say they know you.

DE QUADRA: Men under interrogation will say anything.

WALSINGHAM picks up the dossier which he brought in with him.

WALSINGHAM: Then do you know Anthony Babington?

DE QUADRA: No.

WALSINGHAM: Now that is passing strange. For here are letters to him in your hand.

He adds the dossier to the others.

ELIZABETH: Well sir, is the answer heavy yet?

DE QUADRA: Too heavy, Madam. I am not a sideboard. (*He drops them.*) And His Majesty my master will not have his Servants mocked. I'll go, and tell him of this strange proceeding.

ELIZABETH: Do de Quadra.

    DE QUADRA *going she arrests him:*

And de Quadra—think us lenient that we let you go.

    DE QUADRA *goes.* ELIZABETH *quietly.*

Ye Gods, Cecil, I think it comes soon.

CECIL: I think so too, Your Grace.

ELIZABETH: What is this Babington?

WALSINGHAM: He is a Catholic Gentleman who plots Your Grace's death on Mary Stuart's behalf.

ELIZABETH: What manner of death has this gentleman provided?

WALSINGHAM: Poison, Madam.

ELIZABETH: Hell and damnation, may I not eat?

    She thinks. She sags. To WALSINGHAM.

What can you show?

WALSINGHAM: Why letters Madam, secret letters, which have passed between them hidden in the backs of books, the soles of shoes—and other guilty tricks!

ELIZABETH: A pox on how they passed—are they proof?

WALSINGHAM: Not proof *pedantic.*

ELIZABETH: Proof is pedantic Walsingham. And Scotland is her son.

CECIL: The King of Scots. It is a very calculating boy Your Grace, and relishes his crown. Your Grace might hint . . .

ELIZABETH: Hint what?

CECIL: That if he proved well-governed in the advent of his mother's death—And if Your Grace were not herself to marry and happily deliver of a child—Your Grace might hint that he might look one day, one distant day, to have the Crown of England too.

ELIZABETH: Oh Cecil, you care for me so thoroughly that you have even made ready my winding sheet.

CECIL: Madam—

ELIZABETH: —Do it—Hint—!

Going, pauses to add:

But hearken Cecil, no more than hint. I may yet prove a freak in Nature. (*To* WALSINGHAM.) And you, my other friend, get proof. Get proof pedantic.

Going again, arrested by:

WALSINGHAM: That is more easy said than done Your Grace!

ELIZABETH: I do not ask that you should do it easily.

She holds him with her eyes, then goes.

CECIL: Now I think you could get proof.

WALSINGHAM: Instruct me sir. Mary Stuart is cunning.

CECIL: But mainly she's courageous. And courage is a passion.

WALSINGHAM: So?

CECIL: What luxuries does she enjoy?

WALSINGHAM: The luxuries the Queen allows her. Her state, her visitors, her daily riding in the park.

CECIL: Well then.

WALSINGHAM: No; deprivation would not quench her courage.

CECIL: No it would inflame it. Passions feed on deprivation. And courage is a flame which, fed enough, will burn the house down in the end. What does she think of her son?

WALSINGHAM: She thinks him loyal and loving.

CECIL: Yes, I think you could get proof.

WALSINGHAM: Davison.

A beat of silence while they wait.

Will you give me authority for this?

CECIL: Oh I think you have it good Francis. If you are not to do it easily, presumably you are to do it hard.

DAVISON enters.

DAVISON: Sir?

WALSINGHAM: Where's Babington?

DAVISON: Still under interrogation sir.

WALSINGHAM: Well tell them not to break his fingers.

DAVISON: Very good sir.

He exits.

CECIL: Why are they not to break his fingers?

WALSINGHAM: Because he is to write.

CECIL: Ah, well sir, I will leave you.

WALSINGHAM: Yes sir, I expect you will.

*They go separately. A stable clock chimes, rustic and melancholy.
NAU enters, an old man now in sloppy slippers. He is carrying a
beer keg which he puts down and anxiously regards, drumming his
fingers on it. MARY enters, older too, without head-dress or ruff,
keys and scissors hanging from her waist and carrying an embroidery
frame. She walks slowly and sits.*

MARY: Claud, is it hot or cold today? I cannot tell. Even the
weather here prevaricates. What would I not give for one day
of honest French weather?

She notes his preoccupation.

What is it Claud; are you troubled?

NAU: Nay what should trouble me?

Looks over her shoulder at her work.

Unless the fine embroidered scarf which was to have been
mine last Christmas. And I see has made no progress since the
Spring.

MARY: The heron had no legs last Spring.

NAU (*peering*): His legs are something insufficient now.

MARY: There was an excellent slave-master lost in you.

A little silence, he glancing again at the keg, she sewing. Then:

MARY: I saw a heron in the Park today. I came so close he
hopped into the air all arsy-varsy and asquawking. But then
he wafted up, and sailed away, right quietly. No marvel birds
do not have souls. If they had souls as well as wings they had
been blessed as angels had they not?

She looks up. Feeling her regard he turns and:

NAU: Madam?

MARY (*putting down her frame*): Nay what a devil *is* it?

NAU: I do not know if I should tell Your Grace.

MARY: Then tell me. And I will tell you if you should have told.

NAU: Look Your Grace—(*crossing to barrel, plucking out the bung*) —there is a place in here.

MARY: A place?

NAU: A leather pocket, and in it, this.

Takes out a folded letter. She holds out her hand for it.

MARY: Well we have seen the like before; though seldom so ingenious . . .

NAU: Read it Madam; it's from Babington.

MARY (*more interested*): Oh. (*Reads.*) 'Your Grace, I have acquainted these with the design you know of: Westmorland, Darcy, Cumberland, Arundel, Hamilton—' Hamilton?— good—

NAU: Read on.

MARY: 'They are ready to join it, but only on Your Grace's sure approval. Your Grace's signature to this sets fire to the fuse . . .' (*Slowly.*) My signature to this . . .

NAU: Yes Your Grace.

MARY: 'Else all fails. Your Grace's humble loving servant, Anthony' . . . Nay this is something too ingenious . . . Did that come from the castle brewery?

NAU: I do not know.

MARY: Is this his hand?

NAU: I cannot tell.

They peer together at the paper. She murmurs:

MARY: Nor I . . . I have ruined my eyes, on your poxy scarf . . .

A noise off. She folds the paper quickly; he quickly puts the barrel on the floor.

WALSINGHAM *enters. He takes an arrogant stand and looks at her.* (*Stares, astonished.*) What—? (*Calls.*) Roget!

WALSINGHAM: I have instructed your people to let us alone.

MARY: And who the devil might you be sir to instruct my people?

WALSINGHAM: My name is Walsingham.

MARY *freezes. Then steadily, mildly:*

MARY: Welcome Sir Francis. You are most timely.

WALSINGHAM: Indeed?

MARY: Yes, for I desire your opinion of this keg of beer.

WALSINGHAM: Of what—?

MARY: This keg of beer, sir. Taste it, for I think it tastes oddly.

WALSINGHAM: Madam I am not so junior nor have come so far for nothing weightier than to taste your beer—

MARY: —Yet taste it. For I think it tastes of leather.

WALSINGHAM (*frowns, gives it up, shrugs*): Look lady don't think to beguile me with some little arbitrary wantonness as if to say that you were nothing worse than childish. I know you what you are. Here Madam, letters for you.

Thinking over his evident indifference to the keg, she picks up the packet he throws down. She sees the letters blatantly opened and thinks hard again before, cautiously, flatly:

MARY: Walsingham, these letters have been opened.

WALSINGHAM: Henceforth all your letters will be opened. For I have opened those which you have dropped at certain times and certain places, riding in the Park.

MARY: I have dropped no letters, riding in the Park.

WALSINGHAM: You lie.

Her head flies round and NAU *exclaims.*

It is not worth a quarrel. You will ride no more.

MARY *appalled.*

Nor walk outside these rooms.

MARY: . . . Nay let me understand you, sir—

WALSINGHAM: I have a poor opinion of your understanding Madam, but it should suffice for this—you are to be confined!

NAU: You are not serious?

WALSINGHAM: Who's this?

NAU: I am Her Grace's secretary, sir—

WALSINGHAM: —Then hold your tongue—(*Turning again to* MARY.)

MARY: He is my secretary and my friend!

WALSINGHAM: Still let him hold his tongue. For I have also read the letters which your friends have carried hence when they have visited. In consequence of which henceforward you will have no visitors.

NAU: No visitors—!

WALSINGHAM: And three servants only—

NAU: Three sir—?

WALSINGHAM: Of my choosing. There is another thing—

MARY (*gripping the arms of her chair*): What thing is that?

WALSINGHAM (*pointing to the Cloth of State*): That thing—It comes down.

MARY: . . . Walsingham, come here.

He stands before her.

Do you tell me that I am to be mewed up and deprived of all my retinue?

WALSINGHAM: I do.

MARY: Then you have done your office, get you gone. (*Points to the Cloth of State.*) That stays!

WALSINGHAM: Nay don't attempt the Queen with me—

NAU: —Attempt, sir—Do you dare?

WALSINGHAM (*looking at* MARY): Why what's to dare? Her State's all gone, and God knows in herself I see no Majesty.

Satisfied by her reaction:

Now I'm for London (*Going.*) where I have material matters to attend to.

He goes, briskly. NAU, *tremulous with shock and pity:*

NAU: Oh Madam . . .

She holds up her hand. Her face is white and twisted but not wild.

MARY: Now am I learning self command or losing self-respect? Time was I'd rather have been crucified than sit and suffer censure from a Jack in Office such as that—!

The memory of it gets her to her feet.

An unqualitied, dull cypher such as that! (*Controls herself.*) But no, good Jack, I think this persecution is too gross, too arbitrary—and too hellishly well aimed!

NAU: Madam?

MARY: You know me well. Would you not use me, point by
point as he has done, if you desired me to do something
desperate?

On the last word she produces the letter. NAU, *horrified:*

NAU: Oh Madam, burn it!

She considers it a second, then tosses it onto the table.

MARY: Aye . . .

She sits.

He'll do as he has said though, Claud.

NAU: Aye; that was hatred.

MARY: 'T'was worse; he is a Puritan, and that was disapproval.
He'll save my soul by keeping me walled up. Claud if I am
to be kept walled up I think I shall run mad . . . (*She stares
about. Her glance falls on the paper.*) Let's look at that again.

NAU: Nay.

He grabs for it, but she is too quick for him.

MARY: Now I could swear that this is Babington's own hand.

NAU: Oh do not so persuade yourself—That is your death
warrant!

MARY: It could be my release. It's not unlikely that these gentlemen should want my name for such an enterprise. It could
be my release and *her* death-warrant. By God it were a pity
to burn that . . . And what now should I weigh against it?

NAU: Weigh my love against it!

She looks at him and wavers.

Weigh your son against it!

*She looks away from him; she sags; she lets the letter fall from
her fingers onto the table. Then breathes out a terrible sigh and rests
her face upon her hand, eyes covered.*

NAU: Oh my poor Mistress . . .

WALSINGHAM *enters. She rouses, growling.*

MARY: We thought that you had gone sir.

He dumps onto the table the basket that he carries.

Another thing?

He lifts the lid of basket. She goes and face changes, taking from
the basket a selection of child's toys. Voice wavering:
These are the presents, I have sent to my son.

WALSINGHAM: And your letters.

Takes out and dumps down a wad of letters, taped.

MARY: He—?—He has kept them?

WALSINGHAM: He has never received them.

Tilts basket. She takes out two more billets like the first.

MARY: Never received . . .? Small wonder that he never wrote
to *me*!

WALSINGHAM: He has no wish to. Nor to see you. He knows
you.

MARY: He—?

WALSINGHAM: He has been instructed Madam in the manner
of your life; and in the manner of his father's death.

MARY (*whispering, incredulous*): You, have, blackened me?

WALSINGHAM: How blacken black?

MARY: Nay I think this is some practice Master Walsingham;
you would provoke—(*She fawns on him.*)

WALSINGHAM: —Upon my soul it is the truth!

MARY (*incredulous, pleading*): But of all my letters . . . not one?

WALSINGHAM: Madam you have had no communication! . . .
It is my mistress who has played the mother's part.

He goes. NAU *watches in horror and pity as* MARY, *motionless,*
slides helplessly into tears which she makes no attempt to hide and
then her face darkening and her voice shaking with passion:

MARY: Oh she . . . She-ee! . . . Shee-ee! . . . *Elizabeth!*

She speeds to the table and snatches up the pen.

NAU: Oh Madam you will sign away your life!

MARY: Or hers!

NAU: Aye Madam—murder or suicide—think upon your soul!

MARY: Nay God may think on that, it's his! (*Calls.*) Roget!

NAU: Oh what a summing up!

MARY: I have no choice!

NAU: Cowardly Madam—always we have choice!

MARY: What choice—huh? Six rooms, no sky, and after thirty years maybe lie down and quietly die—And she to have my son? Roget!

BREWER *enters. Stands silently.*

MARY: Where is my gentleman?

BREWER: Your gentleman's without Your Grace. He said Your Grace had made complaint about a keg of beer I sent from the brewery.

She points to the keg. He goes, takes out bung, looks in, finds nothing, looks at her, all very deliberate.

MARY: Who are you sir?

BREWER: I am an English Catholic and Your Grace's subject. I am to take a matter from Your Grace to Father Flint in Chesterfield.

MARY: And he to take it where?

BREWER: We are a chain of trust Your Grace. Each knows his neighbour and no more.

MARY: Take it then.

He comes and takes the letter she holds out, but as he is going back:
But if you take it to Elizabeth—

He spins, indignant:

BREWER: —Nay now you wrong me!

MARY: Be reasonable sir it may be so. And if it is we only ask that you should tell our sister that before we die we'd have one day—nay one half day, of conversation with our son. Ask this of her charity.

BREWER (*angry*): Nay and you suppose I take this to Elizabeth I will not take it anywhere.

MARY (*licks her lips, then*): Sir, I have made my choice. (*Going.*) And you—whatever choice it is that you have made—(*half order, half desperate appeal*)—make haste!

She goes, NAU *following. Enter* WALSINGHAM, CECIL. WALSINGHAM *goes to* BREWER *and takes the letter. Turns as* ELIZABETH *enters slowly dressed in fantastic black. He plonks the letter on the table before her:*

WALSINGHAM: Proof, Your Grace.

    ELIZABETH *looks down at it.* CECIL *puts a document before her.*

CECIL: The warrant, for her execution.

    ELIZABETH *glances unwillingly at it. Then to* BREWER:

ELIZABETH: Did she say anything?

BREWER: She said I was to ask Your Grace if—

ELIZABETH: What? She knew that you would bring this here?

BREWER: She did suspect it Madam; and she said I was to ask—

ELIZABETH: —Nay . . . Then do not tell me what she asked.

    She dips the pen. She licks her lips and looks round for a reprieve.

    To CECIL:

Is there nothing from Scotland?

CECIL: This Your Grace. It is the most discreet, far-sighted child I ever met.

    She takes the letter which he gives her and waves them all off.

    Alone, she looks at the letter. Looks up from it and:

ELIZABETH: Oh; little boy . . .

    She puts down the letter, takes up the pen and signs, calling:

Davison!

    DAVISON *enters, in black.*

Do you see that?

    DAVISON *looks at the signed warrant.*

DAVISON: I see it Your Grace.

ELIZABETH: What will you do with it?

DAVISON: I will take it to Sheffield, Your Grace.

ELIZABETH: You will do it without authority and I shall put you in the Tower for it.

DAVISON: May I know for how long, Your Grace?

ELIZABETH: Until such time as the world recognizes that it was not my desire.

DAVISON: I do not think the world will be deceived by this Your Grace. (*A flick of resentment.*) Nor by Your Grace's mourning.

She looks at him fathomless, then:

ELIZABETH: The world is deceived by nothing. The world must be given something by which to seem to be deceived ... Well sir, do it.

She mounts towards the throne. DAVISON *picks up warrant, and then:*

DAVISON: I think you burden me too much Your Grace. Your Grace must tell me what to do.

ELIZABETH: Why, man—your office!

Drums, cloth of state eclipsed by black cloth of mourning. Two black clad SERVANTS *unroll a black carpet. Enter* MARY, ATTENDANTS, NAU, PRIEST, *all in black.* MARY *stands at the head of the carpet and looks along it, head high but held sideways as though unable to look directly at what is at the end of it, off stage.*

MARY: So there they are, the axe and block. How practical they look. (*To* NAU.) Love, you have stayed with me long. Spare yourself this last?

NAU: An' it please Your Grace, I'll stay a little longer yet.

MARY: Here then; a memento of my idleness; your still unfinished scarf.

Taking it, he breaks down.

Hush now!

DAVISON: Are you ready, Madam?

MARY (*formal*): I claim God's fatherly protection for my son; and Christ's incomprehensible compassion for my soul.

ALL: Amen.

MARY: I'm ready now sir.

She moves but DAVISON *kneels quickly before her.*

DAVISON: Pardon.

MARY: For what?

DAVISON: Your Grace, I brought the warrant.

He looks up at her. She frowns.

MARY: Is it not Davison?

DAVISON: Your Grace.

She touches his hair absently.

MARY: Be comfortable William. The thing you brought was nothing much. A death-warrant requires a royal signature. And I signed my own.

She moves, looks off again at the axe and block, isolated.

And if your Great and Virgin Queen should wonder why I signed it, you are to tell her this: There is more living in a death that is embraced than in a life that is avoided across three score years and ten. And I embrace it—thus!

She throws off the black revealing scarlet head to foot.

Davison.

DAVISON: Madam?

MARY: Now.

Plunges off along the carpet. They tumble after, taken by surprise. Drum beat. Stops convulsively. CECIL *enters. Looks at* ELIZABETH, *cautiously.*

ELIZABETH: She was an adulterous, disorderly, lecherous, strumpet!

CECIL: Yes Your Grace.

ELIZABETH: She was a *fool*!

CECIL: Yes Your Grace.

ELIZABETH: She was—Nay there are no words for saying she was. Only words for saying what she was not.

CECIL *approaches the foot of the throne. Seriously, persuasively:*

CECIL: As: worthy; thoughtful; self-denying; diligent; prepared.

She looks at him attentive, mistrustful.

Your Grace, next year or the next, Spain sends against us his Invincible Armada. And we shall astonish them! And as their great ships founder and they drown they will cry out: 'How? How is this possible?' And our cannon will tell them: 'Elizabeth! Elizabeth made it possible!' And they will hear it across Europe in Madrid—!—Aye Madam they will hear it across Europe—and down Centuries.

In the ringing silence left by his rhetoric her voice comes hard and dead.

ELIZABETH: Very like, Master Cecil; very like . . .
> *She almost snarls:*
And then?
> *She rises painfully, and makes towards Exit. A triumphant fanfare. She ignores it.*

THE CURTAIN FALLS